Blended Families
An Anthology

Edited and compiled by

Valerie L. Coleman

Published by

Pen Of The Writer, LLC
PMB 175
5523 Salem Avenue
Dayton, Ohio 45426
Penofthewriter.com

Published by

Pen Of The Writer, LLC

PMB 175
5523 Salem Avenue
Dayton, Ohio 45426

Library of Congress Control Number: 2006930539

ISBN-13: 978-0-9786066-0-2
ISBN-10: 0-9786066-0-4

Cover design by Candace Cottrell of CCWebDev
Author photo by Melvin Williams of In His Majesty's Image

To Craig,
My husband, my friend, my rock.

To Jesus,
My Husband, my Friend, my Rock.

These things I have spoken unto you, that in Me you might have peace. In the world, ye shall have tribulation: but be of good cheer, I have overcome the world.
~ John 16:33

When you pray for rain, you have to deal with the mud too.

~ West Indian Proverb

Acknowledgments

How do I thank everyone that has supported me over the years on one page? Make a list and ask forgiveness for inadvertent omissions.

- My Craig.
- My handsomes: Lamarr (Mister) and LaShawn (Super) Lewis.
- My Coleman-Pattillo babies.
- My parents: Laura (Mema) and George McDole, Robert (Bebe) and Ann Lewis.
- My sister, Deena (Out) and her husband, Mark Miller.
- My nieces: Aisha (Punkin' Little), Charisse (Chunky Cheeks), Connie, Marketa and Tamiracle.
- My nephew, Marcus Aurelius – Marcus the King.
- My daughter-in-love, Joy, and grandson, Jaylen Burley.
- My God babies: Tranel (Boogie), Aaron and Marnisha.
- My daughters: Ronelle Kinney and Nina Jennings.
- My pastors: Paul and Keisha Mitchell and Bishop Marva Mitchell.
- My friends and supporters: Lucinda Greene (my third best), Sheree Welch, Lisa Vaughn, Gwendolyn Cox, Karen Townsend, Marion Witcher, Melvin Williams (photographer), Rhonda Bogan (publicist), Vanessa Miller, Robert Tann, Ralonda Holt, Julia Scholz-Pinger, Ronnie Harper, Khanh Nguyen, Gayle Simmons, Thad Smith, Greg Parker, Frank Muhammad and Stephane Williams.
- My literary circle of friends: Kendra Norman-Bellamy (author), Avalon Betts-Gaston (attorney), Lynnette Khalfani (author), Wendy Beckman (editor), Sylvia Hubbard (author), Lynel Johnson Washington (editor), Candace Cottrell (graphic designer), Tanya Bates (author) and of course the anthology contributors.

Thank you for your encouraging words, advice and prayers.

iii

Table of Contents

v

Introduction

For thirteen years, I struggled to parent five children from three different households. I instilled respect into my two biological sons and assumed the same respect would be honored by my husband's children. At times, the frustration overwhelmed me. Without the support of family and friends, my marriage would have failed.

After sharing our experience, I decided to compile this book to provide practical tools and biblical principles to successfully blend families. This anthology is composed of personal essays and three fictional accounts. Since blended families are prevalent throughout the Word, two of the fiction stories are based on biblical families. I chose the abstract cover design to depict family relationships by bloodline and blending.

I now realize that I was set-up from the beginning. All of my heartaches, frustrations and sleepless nights were the labor pangs required to birth this book. The struggle revealed things in me that were not pleasing to God and in the process developed my character. Like the woman with the issue of blood, I have touched the hem of His garment and been made whole. I pray that this book ministers to you and your family, as it did ours.

Blessings,

Valerie L. Coleman

A Wiser Man
By Valerie L. Coleman

A wise man learns from his own mistakes.
A wiser man learns from the mistakes of others.
~Proverbs 1:5; 9:9

Fast approaching thirty years old, I knew all the statistics about the availability of eligible bachelors. So I sought the Lord for a husband. I made my requests known to Him, family and friends. I figured that if two, three or fifty people touched and agreed, the Lord was sure to give me the desire of my heart.

"Lord, I acknowledge You as the head of my life. You set the sun and stars in the sky. You put the earth in motion. You are great, kind and merciful. You are awesome. Your ways are faithful, honorable, holy and righteous. Your grace is sufficient. Father, You are my source and my sustainer. You are my peace and my joy.

"Now Lord, You already know what I'm about to ask. Please, send my husband. I need a man that will serve You with all of his heart. I need him to love my boys and me unconditionally. You said that the man that does not work does not eat, so I need a man with a job. And Father, to be sure that I recognize him, let him have kids too. I want to see how he interacts with them to make sure that he'll be good to Lamarr and LaShawn. In the matchless name of Your precious Son. In the name of Jesus. Amen."

Just as I asked, the Lord blessed me with an awesome man. He came to my front door, the friend of a friend. My niece, Aisha, had spent a couple of days with me. When her father,

Eddie, came to take her home, he brought his friend, Craig Coleman, with him. An hour earlier, two of my girlfriends had stopped by for a visit. Engaged in our conversation, I didn't pay Mr. Coleman any attention. While Eddie got Aisha's overnight bags ready, Craig sat quiet in the family room. Ten minutes afterward, I kissed my niece and the trio departed.

A week later, I spoke on the phone with a good friend and prayer partner. "Barb, girl, the Lord has somebody for both of us."

"I know He does. We are His children and He has nothing but good thoughts and plans for our lives."

"Hey, you want to go on another three-day fast?"

"Yeah, we need to get back in His face and the—," the call waiting tone interrupted.

"Hold on, Barb. I've got a call coming in on the other line." I clicked over. "Hello?"

"Hello. May I speak to Valerie?" The sexy voice caught my attention.

"Speaking."

"Hi, Valerie. This is Craig. You remember me, right? We met the other day."

"Craig?" My eyes rolled up, as I tried to remember meeting a Craig. "I'm sorry, but can you jog my memory?"

"I came to your house the other day with Eddie, Aisha's dad."

"Oh, hold on for a second." I clicked back to Barb. "Girl, let me let you go. I got a man on the other line, and I didn't give him my number. I'll call you later. Bye."

The next week, Craig cooked dinner for the boys and me. He bought all the groceries and prepared a succulent steak and potato meal. Needless to say, the courtship ensued.

He filled my emotional love tank with his acts of service, affirming words and gentleness. He lavished me with flowers, candy and shopping money. He worked hard and played harder. He had a beautiful daughter and a cute miniature replication son. We spent quality time together as one big happy family. Hooked.

We met in August. He asked me to be his girlfriend in September. He proposed in October. I accepted in November (it took a few weeks to get my custom-made engagement ring).

With wedding plans underway, the problem solver in me kicked into high gear. To ease my mind, I quizzed my fiancé.

"Okay, now how much is your monthly child support?"

"I'm paying $350 a month, but only $50 of it is actually support. The rest is arrearage."

"Yeah, I know about that back child support. Lamarr and LaShawn's father is about twelve grand in the hole. At $2,500, the delinquency was added to his credit report. I hoped it would jump start the payments, but it didn't." I offered him a glass of lemonade. "How did you end up with an arrearage?"

"With the ex sick and on welfare, she had to make a choice. Either have the county pick up her medical expenses, get food stamps and a small monthly stipend or get reduced medical coverage and court-ordered support from me. The food stamps and stipend weren't enough for her and the kids, but she really needed the insurance. So together we decided that she would take the full insurance and not file for child support. Instead, I gave her money directly. I thought that I'd be doing her and the kids a favor."

"Sounds right to me. Why should it matter that you paid her or the agency? The money is going to the same family."

"Well, it made a big difference to the agency. After her treatments were over, she filed for support as we had agreed.

3

The agency expected me to offset the taxpayer expense and they requested back support for those three years. I ended up owing $6,700."

"How much?"

"Uh," he hesitated to reply. "A little more than $6,000. I kept all the money order stubs and cancelled checks as proof of payment. But when I contacted the agency, the case worker told me that unless the ex would admit to receiving government assistance and money from me, I didn't have a case."

"Why is that?"

"Because that constitutes welfare fraud and she'd have to pay it all back. She'll never admit to getting the money."

"So where do we go from here?"

"The money I paid to her directly is considered a gift, so I have to pay the arrearage."

"So basically, **we** have to pay twice."

"Yeah."

"Wow." I noticed the concern that crawled onto Craig's face. "It's okay, babe. At $300 a month, the arrearage will be paid off in about two years." With that matter resolved, I posed my next question. "Now what about bills? Do you have anything outstanding that we need to work through?"

"Other than my car payment, I don't have any bills."

"Great." I expelled a sigh of relief. "Now where are your divorce papers?" I loved this man and wanted to be sure that when I said, "I do," I'd be his only wife. I've never been much for sharing men and besides, polygamy is a crime.

~ ~ ~ ~ ~ ~ ~

Two months before the wedding, Craig received a letter from the Child Support Enforcement Agency (CSEA). He came by the house to share the not-so-good news.

"Hey, Beautiful," my husband said as he landed a big fat wet one on me.

"Hey, Handsome. How was your day?"

"It was okay, until I picked up the mail."

"What's wrong?" He dropped his head and handed me an open letter. "The devil!" I plopped onto the couch. "I thought the $300 was taking care of the arrearage. Why did they seize your income tax return?"

"They seize any lump-sum payment or bonus when the arrearage is more than $500. The agency is linked directly with the IRS and my employer." He paused. "I am so sorry."

"Well, there goes our honeymoon. The balance is due in two weeks and I've wiped out everything for the wedding." I stood and walked into the kitchen. "Nothing we can do about it now."

After our July ceremony, we tried to settle into a life of normalcy. We received another letter from the CSEA. In our county, if the custodial parent is on government assistance, the case is reviewed every three years. Craig had to submit tax forms for the last three years, proof of residency and four recent pay stubs. A few weeks later, we got another letter. The monthly support was being adjusted. As an engineer, I thrive on facts. Since all the legal mumbo jumbo on the documents had my head swimming, we had to consult an attorney. Five-hundred dollar retainer. Although I did not care for the situation, I learned a lot about the system.

"In reviewing your records, I see that your monthly payment includes $50 for arrearage and another —"

"No ma'am." I interjected. "The monthly support is $50. The rest is for arrearage."

"Well, let me look again." She flipped through the papers and tapped her Cross pen on the desk. "No, actually the support is $300 and they want to increase it by fifty percent. With the increase and the $50 arrearage, your monthly support will be $500."

Gulp. "So, you're telling me that instead of $50 a month for the next thirteen years, our payment is $500?" Now, I believe with all my heart that a man that fathers a child is responsible for the emotional and financial need of that child. And the Bible states it quite clearly in I Timothy 5:8, but it just wasn't fair. We had all this money going out and couldn't get a dime from my boys' biological father. And believe me, I tried. His occupation as a clergy made it difficult to garnish his wages. Bummer.

"Well, there's also a monthly fee assessed by the agency for handling the account." She saw the worry etched on my face. "It's only two percent." She pulled a document out of the massive stack. "Hmm. This is peculiar."

"What now?" Craig asked.

"The agency is giving you the option to carry insurance for the children or allow the county to pick it up. If you choose to carry the insurance, they'll reduce the monthly support by your increase in premium. Do you know how much that would be?"

"About $30," I said without hesitation. I had just completed the insurance enrollment process. "So the net effect is zero. The premium goes up by $30 and the support goes down by $30."

"Exactly," the attorney said.

As the Coleman money manager, I needed all the specifics. "Now let me ask you this, who handles deductibles and co-pays?"

"Well, since she's on welfare, she's only responsible for the first $100 per year. You'd be responsible for the rest."

"So if she decided to get braces for the kids, we'd have to pay any outstanding balances?"

"That's right."

"Even if the insurance only covered one-fourth?"

"Uh-huh."

"We'll go with the county plan," Craig and I said in unison.

With fifteen minutes left in our session, I asked for an explanation of support calculations. "What happens with the support amount if the ex goes back to work? It'll go down, right?"

"Actually, just the opposite. The support is calculated based on the total income of the biological parents. Let's say, for example, that your husband earned $70,000 per year and his ex-wife earned $30,000. Their total combined income is $100,000. The agency uses a factor to determine the child's standard of living based on the total income. We'll estimate it at $20,000."

"Okay, so far I'm with you."

"Good." She turned the computer monitor around, so that we could read the screen. "Now at $20,000 annual assistance for the children, Craig would be responsible for seventy percent."

"Because I made seventy percent of the total income?"

"Yes. That equates to $14,000 per year. The remaining $6,000 is the thirty percent that your ex-wife would be responsible to handle." She spun the screen back around. "So, if you get paid every week, the $14,000 is divided by 52 weeks to get your weekly support. The agency would garnish your pay check by about $269 a week."

"Plus the two percent fee," I added.

"You've got it. The agency will deduct the court-ordered support from your paycheck until the child is emancipated."

"Emancipated?" Details. I need details.

"Basically, you will pay the support until the kids graduate from high school, drop out of school or reach eighteen years old."

"What if the arrearage is not paid off at the time of emancipation?"

"Arrearages are not dismissed with emancipation. That money will continue to be deducted until it's paid in full. But if you have a significant drop in income, you can request a decrease in support."

"One of my college friends lives in Michigan." I said, as I shifted in the plush leather chair. "She told me that when her husband's ex-girlfriend filed for child support, they included her income too. Is that right?"

"Possibly. Each state has laws that govern the family courts and child support calculations." She shut down the computer and stuffed papers in her brief case. "Hate to run, but I've got a court appearance in fifteen minutes. Please stop by the receptionist's desk to settle your account. I'll see you in a few weeks. Don't worry. Everything will be fine."

Just as we finalized the local order of support, we received another notice. After six months of long-distance phone calls and another $500 for legal representation, our total outgoing monthly support increased to almost $800. And still nothing coming in from the clergy.

When all was said and done, we were left with just enough money to keep the payment on Craig's Toyota Corolla current. Not at all what we had discussed or planned. As a single mother, I had struggled for twelve years to provide for my boys. I had hoped to have a release from some of my financial burden, but that didn't happen.

Prior to our relationship, Craig and I had both filed bankruptcy. My situation resulted from ignorance. I co-signed for a car loan without understanding the impact if the payments were not made. So to avoid the bank forcing me into foreclosure, I filed Chapter 13 to keep a roof over my babies' heads.

Craig was in the military when he divorced. He had just been called out to the Gulf War in Iraq. Given his distance from the soon-to-be ex-wife, he was advised to file bankruptcy to protect his assets. Good advice.

A few months into our marriage, we received a barrage of delinquent notices. Apparently, Craig's bankruptcy was not discharged and the creditors came a-calling.

As the Coleman CFO, I contacted each creditor to make arrangements for payment. Most of them accepted my offer to take half, given they received the money within four weeks. When I entered into this covenant of marriage, I meant it. So instead of walking out, I drained my savings and dug into my retirement to pay off thousands of dollars in debts that were incurred during his first marriage. I must really love this man.

Unbeknownst to me, settlements on accounts are considered income. During the next tax season, the IRS sent us a letter indicating that we owed $1,000 for the taxes, penalty and interest associated with negotiating reduced payments. Man, can we get a break?

~ ~ ~ ~ ~ ~ ~

As a penny pincher, I prepared our income tax returns. No sense paying an accountant a few hundred dollars to work up the numbers. In 1995, I filed my first joint return. Unclear as to the tax laws regarding child support and claiming deductions for non-residential children, I called 800.TAX.1040 for assistance.

"I don't see where to claim the support payments on the tax form. Is it a Schedule A deduction?"

"No ma'am," Representative 1245903 said. "Per Publications 17 and 504, child support payments are not deductible."

"Oh," I contorted my lips to the left. "Well, my husband is the non-custodial parent, so how do I handle the deduction for his children?"

"If he has a divorce decree, it will specify who can claim the children. Some states require parents to alternate years; other states only allow the custodial parent to claim the children. Do you have a copy of the decree?"

"Yes, I do, but I don't really understand all that legal jargon. This document is about fifteen pages long."

"Well, somewhere in the document, you'll find a clause that states visitation, support and income tax deductions."

I rifled through the papers, until I found the information. "Okay, this says that he can claim the youngest child and she can claim the oldest. But she doesn't work. So how can she file a tax return?"

"She can't."

"So what happens to the other deduction?"

"If no one claims the other child, the deduction is forfeited. You can request that the custodial parent complete Form 8332."

"I'm not familiar with that form."

"Form 8332 is the File Release of Claim of Exemption for Children of Divorced or Separated Parents form. The custodial parent can allow the non-custodial parent to claim the children for the current tax year or future years."

"Really? Would you please mail me a copy of that document?"

"Yes ma'am." After verifying our address, Representative 1245903 said, "You'll receive the form and instruction booklet in about two weeks."

"Thank you."

Now that was good information. Since we couldn't write off the support payments, we could recoup some of our expense by claiming both children. It only made sense. Well, it made sense to us.

"I spoke with some of my friends and they said that it was illegal for you to claim both kids," the ex explained to Craig and me.

"I called the IRS directly. The rep told me that as long as you completed this form, everything was okay."

"Well, I'm not comfortable doing that. I need to talk to my case worker."

"Your case worker?" My eyes widened to the size of two hard-boiled eggs. "Why do you need to contact your case worker? Since Craig gave you money directly, we've been stuck with paying that $6,700 twice."

"He didn't give any money directly."

"Oh, okay." I looked at Craig, then back at the ex. "We're really not trying to get over on you."

"So when should we expect to hear back from you?" Craig asked.

"Give me a week. I should know something by then."

A week turned into two. We needed that money ASAP. "Babe, have you heard from the ex about claiming both kids?"

"No. I need to give her a call." After a lengthy telephone debate, the results were in. "She's not going to let us claim my daughter. She said that her case worker told her not to."

"But that doesn't make any sense. She's not losing out on anything. We've had to pay double on the arrearage, can't claim the support and you've been available to the kids for anything else they needed." Exasperated, I expelled a deep breath and shook my head. "Why won't she do this one thing for us?"

"I don't know."

We visited another attorney and spent another $300 for his retainer. "Lots of times this becomes an attempt to get money out of you."

"I don't get it," I said, as I took a seat.

"Well, she may hold out on allowing you to claim the child so that you'll give her some money. I see this tactic a lot with welfare recipients."

"You've got to be kidding me." I crossed my legs and leaned forward. "So we have to pay her to allow us to claim a child that she can't claim because she doesn't work?"

"Uh-huh."

"But she wouldn't sign the form. We already tried," my loving king said.

"How much would you be willing to give her to claim the child?"

"I don't know. I think we'd get back an extra $400, if we claim six dependents instead of five."

"Okay. I'll start with $100 and offer her no more than $300. How's that sound?"

"I guess that'll work."

About three weeks later, our only daughter called in a hysterical fit. "Daddy, why are you taking me away from Mommy? I don't want to live with you."

"Baby, what are you talking about?"

"Mommy said that you are making me come live with you. I want to stay here."

Tears cascaded down my husband's cheeks. "Put your mother on the phone."

Only able to hear one side of the conversation, I surmised her comments.

"Don't raise your voice at me."

"But why would you get our eight-year-old daughter involved in grown folks' business?" I handed him a tissue.

"Well why would you try to take her from me?"

"Nobody's trying to take her from you. Did you even read the paper or call the attorney?" He blew his nose and continued. "All we're trying to do is claim her since you can't."

"Well I have to go to his office next week and I do not appreciate this harassment."

"We are not trying to harass you. All we're asking for is a little help. It won't cost you anything."

A couple of days passed. Craig's aunt rebuked him for creating so much confusion. Once he explained the whole story, her tone mellowed. A week later, the attorney called me. "She was offended that I offered her any money."

"Really?"

"She said that she would have signed the form without having to involve an attorney."

"Humph. Now what?"

"I'll draft up an amendment to the divorce decree. It will allow you to claim your husband's daughter as long as his ex does not work for six consecutive months in any given year. You'll have to include a copy of this amendment with your tax returns."

"That's not a problem. Thanks for your help."

I filed the returns without a day to spare. When the letter from the IRS came in the mail, I assumed that the plain white envelope meant the return was filed joint versus head of household. Boy, was I wrong.

"They seized the return!" I dropped my purse on the floor, as my eyes darted back and forth across the paper. I called the IRS again. "But how can they take my money? Part of the return was from my earnings before we even got married."

"Yes ma'am, I understand. However, with the arrearage and the joint filing status, the IRS has no way of determining how much of the return belongs to you."

"So I should file head of household next year?"

"No, you can't file head of household because you're married. You can do married filing separate."

"But that reduces the amount of my return."

"Yes ma'am it probably will. Your only other option is to submit Form 8379 as an injured spouse. It's a two-page document that includes a break down of each person's portion of income and deductions. Based on the information, we will determine how much of the return will be applied to the arrearage and how much will be issued to you."

"Okay. Please mail me a copy of the form."

"Yes ma'am. You'll receive the form and instruction booklet in about two weeks."

"Thank you."

With my newfound knowledge, I filed the 1995 return as recommended. A copy of the amended divorce decree and the Injured Spouse form were included. Several weeks later, guess what. The return was seized. After several conversations with IRS reps, I learned that the Injured Spouse form was overlooked. And since the money was applied to the arrearage, it could not be recovered.

The next year, I attached the Injured Spouse form to the front of our ever-growing tax documents. With a bright yellow marker, I highlighted the form name and number. Since these claims go before a special review committee, the return was delayed. But in early July, we received the money. Bless the Lord!

~ ~ ~ ~ ~ ~ ~

Through all the financial fiery darts, God's grace was sufficient. We found a new church home at Revival Center Ministries, International and received a revelation on tithes and offerings. With our hearts touched, we stretched ourselves and paid $400 a month. The sick calf. The rejected offering. As we turned our finances over to the Lord and trusted Him with our money, we increased our giving to ten percent of our net. A little more faith, a little more giving. We continued to grow our seed and gave ten percent of our gross earnings. Without missing a beat, we now pay almost fifteen percent of our gross earnings. We didn't have a major win fall; we just gave it over to Him.

Today, our credit has been restored. We paid our bills on time and participated in a class sponsored by City Wide Development. With the help of our instructor, Dee Severs, we corrected errors on our credit reports. One year later, our reports were clean and our credit rating had improved. Time to go to the lender. We submitted letters of explanation for our bankruptcies and within two weeks, we were approved. As we've continued to give God His honor and pay our bills on time, every time, our credit ratings soared to almost 800.

Oh yeah, we spent five days in Montego Bay, Jamaica for our honeymoon. God is faithful!

~ ~ ~ ~ ~ ~ ~

With 20/20 hindsight, we realized that our first year of blending would have gone a bit smoother if we had taken the time to accurately assess our finances. You will not be able to eliminate every financial hardship, but preparation to minimize the impact is an exercise of wisdom. Save yourself some frustration by doing the following:

- Pay your tithes and offerings from your gross income. My pastor, Paul O. Mitchell, is writing a series of books about grace giving. The revelation on New Testament giving changed our lives.

- Survey other blended families. Find out what worked for them and what they wished they had done differently. How did they address visitation? Vacations? Discipline? Finances? Holidays? The other parent?

- Pull your credit reports from the three main bureaus and review them together (and annually thereafter). If neither of you are credit-report savvy, contact a financial planner. Joshua Johnson of Grace Financial is an excellent resource (Grace-Financial.com). Free annual reports can be requested by calling 877.322.8228 or visiting AnnualCreditReport.com. You can also request your report by writing to

  > Annual Credit Report
  > PO Box 105281
  > Atlanta, GA 30348-5281

- Contact the Child Support Enforcement Agency (CSEA) and request a statement to verify monthly support payments, arrearages, etc.

- Understand the laws governing your CSEA and support calculations. What happens if the non-custodial parent is in the military? What if the non-custodial parent is self-employed or a full-time clergy? What if the non-custodial parent lives out of state? How will new additions to your family, either by birth or adoption, affect child support?

- Call the IRS at 800.TAX.1040 with questions about deductions, exemptions and other tax concerns.
- Obtain a copy of the divorce decree and keep it in safe place.
- And oh my God! Alimony! Be sure to understand how much is required and for how long. Was future money included (retirement, bonuses, insurance)?

Although the adjustment may not be easy, if you plan ahead, communicate daily with your mate and develop a consistent prayer life, your family will survive and thrive.

Nothing New Under the Sun

By Dr. Vivi Monroe Congress

"Every man gets to choose his destiny, no matter what his father did [or did not do]."
— Bernie Mac, from the movie, *Guess Who*

So you've found the person that completes you, your better half, "the one." Because of them, you're more productive, focused, invincible even. Sparks fly each time your eyes meet, alarms sound when you touch and a chorus of angels croon your very own celestial theme song when you kiss. In each other's presence, you feel an effortless peace and quiet knowing; in one another's absence, your day is, at best, abysmal. Mutual respect, balance and support are always the "special of the day" between the two of you — and then, generally speaking, somewhere between the third and sixth month of dating the music comes to a grinding halt, silencing the enthusiastic chirping of birds and all things "somewhere over the rainbow."

As it has always been with that which holds promise, several issues can and do introduce complication and impediment — otherwise known as challenges — often thwarting the opportunity for true development of the best relationships. Obstacles to these amorous unions are not too different from an obstacle strewn in the road; both can annihilate forward acceleration. You'll find yourself faced with either having to figure out a best method for maneuvering around it or in some cases, removing it altogether to avoid heartaches in the long run. Either way, you're expending energy in thought or action to progress and reach your desired destination. In this case, a healthy and prosperous relationship.

<u>Defining Blend(ed) / Family / Blended Family</u>

Scores of dating relationships, engagements and even marriages are adversely impacted by and often succumb to the devastating effects of SIDS — Stagnancy, Intrusion, Distortion and eventually Silence. The causes of SIDS can vary; however, contributions are frequently pouring in from donors: people with small minds and big mouths who are often the first to insist that you utilize their unsolicited personal experiences as the measuring tool for your relationship; well-meaning (and sometimes not) parents and in-laws-to-be who have great difficulty seeing the bigger picture, but have no difficulty whatsoever sharing their snapshot of your future; and a myriad of other "well-wishers" engaging in similar to worse behavior.

The influence of these SIDS donors can sometimes take their dooming toll on a budding relationship that's just beginning to sprout roots. On the converse, sometimes their input can be central to the establishment of still stronger, deeper roots between the couple. And though there will surely be those true and loyal supporters of your relationship, there will certainly be those who are just not feeling any of it. But even with all that, nothing waves a red flag quite like children — you will have to face the music instead of changing the station.

I'm a firm believer that children possess radar-like, almost second-sight ability, sensing those things that don't readily appear on the surface. Children offer a unique yet accurate take on that which adults opt to glamorize or rationalize into being what we want it to be instead of facing it as it is. With wisdom, your job is to determine what's important, how important it is and most notably, what God is instructing you to do in the matter. And that holds true for anything from romantic relationships to paying bills.

One or both of you may have children from previous relationships. Though these small people love you, they did not sign up for New Relationship 101. Their participation and involvement in your romantic merger is involuntary and laden with reservation born of a hodgepodge of emotions and questions that echo, "What does your fairytale mean for me...me...me?" Though children may not have the first or last word in what ultimately transpires in your relationship, these pint-size personalities should never be underestimated. They have the power to dole out a full-sized blow that can leave a stinging impact on any relationship, bruising it beyond recognition. Therefore, their feelings should never be assumed or overlooked in the well-intentioned process of blending.

Blending a family is a bit more complicated than a mathematical elucidation of yours + mine = ours. No, it's way more than that. Blending is God's way of enriching and enlarging your life by filling it with others who complement the work that He's doing in and will perform through you. The word blend means to mix, merge or combine in a manner such that two or more separate sources become indistinguishable and void of obvious transitions and/or [former] boundaries. This definition is valid and sounds good, but in a quixotic sort of way. When blending a family with the intent to create a new, cooperative unit, you cannot afford to blend in such a restrictive, defined sense, especially not early on — if at all.

Each person's role and place in the family is distinctive and by divine design. No one's individual qualities should ever be sacrificed or tolerated, but respected and celebrated unless, of course, it proves detrimental to the family unit as a whole.

Keep in mind, God accepts each of us into His family just as we are. Though He loves us all equally, He is still willing to love and appreciate us individually and work with us on those traits (behavioral and otherwise) that need polishing.

~ ~ ~ ~ ~ ~ ~

Fascinated, Little Johnny watched as his stepmother smoothed cold cream on her face.

"Why do you do that?" he asked.

"To make myself beautiful," she said, then removed the cream with a tissue.

"What's the matter?" The inquisitive child continued, "Giving up?"

Blending isn't always the joining of two adults with children (while it is the most commonly thought of), but can be demonstrated in an exciting array of combinations: an aunt and uncle taking in their niece and nephew, a single person legally adopting a child, a family that takes in foster children, half-siblings living under the same roof and the list continues.

Biblical Examples of Blended Family Scenarios and Outcomes

> *However, what has been done is what will be done; there is nothing new under the sun.*
> ~ Ecclesiastes 1:9 (Holman Christian Standard)

Biblically speaking, even the blending of families is nothing new. First, let's look at the lives of Sarah, Abraham and Hagar (Genesis 16:1–16). In this scenario, we see instances of mothering, surrogate mothering and step-mothering all in one blended-family narrative. Sarah, regarded as "fair to look upon," was an extremely beautiful woman desired by men of great affluence and influence. Sarah was also barren and unable to conceive children with her husband, Abraham. Her diminishing faith and increasing impatience with God's promise of motherhood resulted in Sarah choosing Hagar, her personal servant, to bear a child for Abraham. Sarah soon realized the error of her decision. When Hagar discovered she was pregnant, she looked down her nose at Sarah. Displeased at the audacity of her servant's contempt, Sarah took a hard approach with Hagar and caused her to run away.

In the end, the stressed out Hagar received a "talking to" from the Lord. As a result, she had to abandon her pride and return in submission to Sarah. Hagar gave birth to Ishmael; however, this son was not the one God promised to Sarah.

Thirteen years later, when Sarah was about ninety years old, she gave birth to Isaac. At a family gathering in honor of this young life, she noticed her stepson, Ishmael, disrespecting and behaving inappropriately toward the baby. Having decided enough was enough, Sarah had Abraham sent Ishmael and his mother packing. This demand undoubtedly put Abraham in a tight spot. He was faced with divorcing himself from his first-born child. Though he conceded, it didn't come easy or without anguish. His actions set in motion the long-standing schism between the Muslims and the Jews. We must be ever sensitive of keeping ourselves in alignment with the will of God because our obedience — or disobedience, in this case — affects not only our lives, but the lives of our children.

Due to the polygamous laws of that time, the blended family concept was not only prevalent but accepted as the norm. Jacob married and fathered children with two sisters, Rachel and Leah — oh, and I can't forget to mention the two additional surrogate mothers (Genesis 29).

The Bible is clear that Jacob loved Rachel more than Leah; however, it does not indicate that he did not love Leah. And though Jacob managed to keep his family intact, one can assume that it was no stroll along the beach. He had to deal with and stretch himself in accordance to the insecurities of two women. Rachel had his heart, but couldn't immediately bear him children. Her infertility consumed her. And Leah, quite fertile, longed for the love that Jacob felt for her sister. Fortunately for Jacob, the two surrogates/servants made no demands...at least not that we know of!

Leah mothered seven children, the number associated with God's completion of a thing. After the birth of Leah's last child, God "remembered" Rachel and opened her womb. In Hebrew, to remember (homologeo) is to acknowledge and in Greek (mnaomai) it means to reward. So, despite Rachel's anxious interference and constant fretting, God still blessed her and gave her the desires of her heart. But He did it in His time and on His terms. When they learned to place their trust securely in God and realized that He alone was able to complete the lack in their lives, Jacob and his very extended family formed the twelve tribes of Israel.

Moses, another prominent biblical figure, was the product of a blended family. He was a Hebrew baby adopted into an Egyptian household, and not just any household, but the Pharaoh's royal family (Exodus 2:1–10).

Pharaoh attempted to establish a warped method of population control. His official command ordered the immediate extermination of all Hebrew male children. To save their newborn son and brother, Moses' mother and sister constructed a waterproof basket. They placed baby Moses inside and sent him floating down the Nile River. He was discovered by Pharaoh's daughter, adopted, and according to Acts 7:22 (NLT), raised and educated in all the wisdom of the Egyptians and was powerful in speech and action. The same

Pharaoh that initiated the death decree came to grandfather Moses relationally and existentially.

Upon reaching manhood and through a series of events that included manslaughter, Moses chose his people and accepted God's assignment as their leader. He guided them from Egyptian enslavement to freedom in the promised land of Canaan.

The most venerated example is Jesus Christ who made His grand and long-awaited entrance into the lives of Mary and His stepfather, Joseph. During their betrothal period, Joseph discovered that Mary was going to have a baby — and he knew he had never been intimate with her. A simple man in love, Joseph wasn't up for scandal or public scrutiny and decided to break his engagement to Mary in secrecy. Assuming Mary's condition was evidence of her unfaithfulness, Joseph, by law, was well within his rights to break it off. But here's the catch, Joseph, a man with true heart and dedication, had been hand picked, chosen, just as Mary, to be a catalyst for ushering in the new covenant God had for His people. The Greek definition of chosen (eklektos) is to be elected, favored, preferred. A powerful testament to the immense integrity of Joseph's character and how much he had impressed the heart of God.

Enlightened by an angel as he slept, Joseph received the details concerning Mary and was dissuaded from jumping ship (Matthew 1:18–25). Armed with spiritual insight and an affinity towards both his woman and his God, Joseph protected Mary, her reputation and our unborn Savior. Joseph gallantly embraced his calling as a father long before he held a baby in his arms. He made sacrificial provisions to ensure Mary's well-being and in all this, Joseph's role remained pivotal in aiding the delivery of God's promise into the earth. He was the kind of stepfather that we unfortunately don't hear much about today in blended-family accounts and the same kind that even many biological fathers should take note to emulate.

In these cases of blending, fulfillment of greater purpose was always at work. These examples speak of the preservation of promise, the character of commitment, and faithful follow-through. Sure, they endured baby-mamma drama, jealousy, favoritism and other issues as well, but to avoid some of their pitfalls, search your heart to determine what work God is trying to do in your life using your blended family. Though God has us intricately and primarily wired for relationship with Him, He also equipped us to relate to one another. He went to great extremes to send His Son, Jesus, as a ransom to secure it.

<u>God's Design and Plan for Family</u>

A frustrated father, whose stepson was always getting into mischief, finally asked him, "How do you expect to get into Heaven?"

The boy thought it over and said, "Well, I'll just run in and out, and in and out, and keep slamming the door until Saint Peter says, 'For Heaven's sake, Johnny, come in or stay out!'"

If the truth were revealed, every earthly mother and father is a stepparent, filling in for the Lord, ministering to a little soul assigned to their care. God views marriage as a covenant and that family is an extension, a blessing of that covenant. But simply because the covenant of family is of God, do not assume that it is never subject to challenge or that it won't experience the storms of life. For this reason, I extend encouragement to those who find themselves being tested. Tests are seasonal and do pass.

If your family is being put to the test, know that in His infinite wisdom, He beckons all who are His: look to Him in all things; let Him lead you; let Him show you. This difficulty that you're facing has a time limit and a purpose yet to be revealed. So, be patient and don't weaken and wander away from Him. Seek Him out for counsel and guidance. Refrain from being faithless by attempting to help Him shoulder your burdens and instead, exercise calm and just listen for His voice; His words He will make plain. Even in the midst of your struggle you will know His voice and you'll hear Him when He speaks. For He is the voice of peace. He is the voice of certainty. He is the voice of truth.

Allow Him to speak and clearly reveal Himself in all of your needs: family, health issues, loss of loved ones, fear, addiction, lack of resources, salvation, unholy alliances. Below is an ideal prayer blueprint to use as a reference when praying on behalf of your family:

To You, O Lord, I lift up [my soul]; in You I trust, O my God. Do not let me be put to shame, nor let [my enemies] triumph over me. No one whose hope is in You will ever be put to shame, but they will be put to shame who are treacherous without excuse. Show [me] Your ways, O Lord, teach [me] Your paths; guide [me] in Your truth and teach [me], for You are God my Savior, and my hope is in You all day long.

~ Psalm 25:1–5 (NIV)

Focus on the words that are enclosed in brackets, insert your personalized requests; include the word "family" or a particular family member and/or issue by name, praying specifically for that which you want God's help.

In Genesis 22, we find Abraham under the tremendous weight of being tested to sacrifice his son. Let us grow from his example.

A. Verses 1–10 The TEST: What is God asking of you? Respond like Abraham, be teachable and open. Receive instructions and act on what He has told you to do.

B. Verses 11–14 The TRIAL: The process of being tested or the experience that tests your strength, faith, and patience. Your ability to stand and face matters is crucial at this juncture.

C. Verses 15–18 The TESTIMONY: God will give you a testimony in exchange for your test. He will validate your victory so you can be a blessing to others in similar situations. Obediently place those loved ones and matters of deep concern on the altar of sacrifice before God. Surrender and submit your will by doing what you can, then move aside and let Him do what you can't. Wait and watch as God provides what you need!

Make positive confessions over your family and life, give attention to where you want to be and release concern over the state you're currently in. You want what you see with your spiritual eye and not your natural sight. To get there, use your God-given authority by speaking things into existence. Express a good report every chance you get, "I am healed," "We are blessed," etc.

No matter what, stay focused and stay faithful! Even if you don't see a way out, God says, "It's there." You say, "I'm afraid." God says, "I'm right here with you." When you try your best to listen, but don't hear a thing, God says, "Oh, but I am speaking." And remember, when you think you're growing impatient, perhaps in that very moment, you're actually growing in patience.

Conclusion

Miss Jones had been giving her second-grade students a lesson on science. She explained magnets and demonstrated how they pick up nails and other bits of iron. Now it was time for testing.

"My name begins with the letter 'm' and I pick up things. What am I?"

Little Johnny in the front row proudly said, "You're a mother!"

In life and in families, challenges will come, but hidden blessings come along with them. Some of life's best lessons arrive through seasonal trials. Though you can never fully prepare for everything that you'll encounter, careful planning and communication is important to the success of a blended family. Create a calendar just for family discussions. Allow all members an opportunity to respectfully express themselves without reservation. Establish a platform that invites opinions and the participation of each family member in the founding of rules and schedules, as well as recognition and appreciation for individual accomplishments.

Know that you'll probably encounter issues ranging from extra bathroom time to money matters. But in a society where one in three Americans is either a stepchild, stepparent or stepsibling and at least one-third of all children are expected to live in a stepfamily before age eighteen, learning how to effectively communicate early can sidestep more serious headaches down the road. Adjustment issues must be expected, but parents should always present a unified front, especially since they are the reason for the blending. In matters pertaining to one another's children, particularly when the news is not good (to the ears of the child, that is), allow the biological parent, with the stepparent present, to deliver the news. This approach diminishes the good guy/bad guy perception and exemplifies your support of one another.

Allow your family to be the fragrance of Christ to God (II Corinthians 2:15) through a consistent and sincere prayer life. Let your family members hear you call each of them by name as you request God's favor on their lives.

Whether you're pondering, preparing for or positioned in a blended family, I pray that your heart be touched to overflowing with joy; a joy that comes from peace; a peace that comes from knowing Him and may knowing Him bring you the wisdom and understanding to guide you and your family always.

Daddy — What a Precious Word!
By Kevin Wayne Johnson

A man shall be satisfied with good by the fruit of his mouth: and the recompense of a man's hands shall be rendered unto him.
~ Proverbs 12:14

As I arrive home from a hard day's work, my sons greet me at the door.

"Daddy! Daddy! Welcome home," they say with joy and tenderness of heart. "Glad to see you, Daddy!"

I cannot explain the pride that wells within me. Nor can I convey the sheer delight of seeing their little faces twinkle, when I enter the house each day.

"How was your day, son?" I make it a point to acknowledge each child individually.

"Good, Daddy," they utter back with confidence. What a precious way to end my day.

As a father, husband, author and preacher of the Gospel of Jesus Christ, my mission is to inspire, encourage and challenge everyone within my sphere of influence. I reinforce the importance of glorifying God, the One who created us.

God birthed us into the world to do His will and fulfill our purpose. As men, fatherhood falls in line with our purpose, whether or not you father a child. Youth observe our lifestyles to distinguish between right and wrong. Our role is to make the eternal, immortal and invisible God evident to them.

"Father" is a noun derived from the Greek word patēr, meaning "a nourisher, protector and upholder." This word is used 963 times in the Bible and its plural appears 522 times. Other forms include "father's" (used 146 times), "fathers'" (used 10 times) and "fatherless" (used 41 times). In addition, 254 references to the heavenly Father, God Almighty, appear in the Scriptures.

Let's expound upon the biblical definition of father.

> <u>Nourisher</u> — to supply with what is necessary for life, health and growth; to cherish or keep alive; to strengthen or promote.

> <u>Protector</u> — to defend or guard from attack, invasion, loss, or insult; to cover; to shield; to provide.

> <u>Upholder</u> — to support or defend; to lift upward, support, or raise; to keep up or keep from sinking.

Abba, an ancient Aramaic word, translates as Father. Jesus used it three times in the New Testament in reference to God. The declaration defines God as a loving, approachable Father.

> *And He said, "Abba, Father, all things are possible unto Thee; take away this cup from Me: nevertheless not what I will, but what Thou wilt."*
> ~ Mark 14:36

Jesus addressed God with the household term for father, unheard of in Palestinian Judaism at that time. It points to Jesus' unique relationship with God, and so it is with the natural father. Because of the exclusive relationship we have with our children, biological or not, they should feel comfortable to approach us at any time, in any situation. Do you create an environment for your children to approach you? Care for your children as God cares for us — His children.

> *For ye have not received the spirit of bondage again to*
> *fear; but ye have received the Spirit of adoption*
> *whereby we cry, Abba, Father.*
> ~ Romans 8:15

The Holy Spirit positions the believer as a son in God's family. Abba is the intimate name that we use to express the relationship with our heavenly Father. When our children call us "Daddy," they are expressing a natural affectionate intimacy toward their earthly father.

The Bible makes no differentiation between the love that a father has for his child, whether by conception, marriage or adoption. Through the Spirit, we are adopted into God's royal family. Likewise, through the natural process of marriage and adoption, we embrace the children as our own. Our ordained role as a father requires that we take proper stewardship over these precious little ones with unconditional love.

> *And because ye are sons, God hath sent forth the Spirit*
> *of His Son into your hearts, crying, Abba, Father.*
> ~ Galatians 4:6

The Holy Spirit is divinely given to every child upon adoption. This same Spirit gives us awareness that God is our Abba Father.

The Word of God is consistent from Genesis to Revelation. Fathers are called to protect, nourish and uphold. When we fulfill this role, our approachable demeanor will make our children comfortable in our presence. They will not be ashamed to cry on our shoulders. They will ask of us their hearts' desires, knowing, that as fathers, we will respond in truth and love.

Be the father God intended and He will surely smile on you. The blessings upon your family will come through you, the conduit and head of your household. YOU ARE A FATHER. Love your ordained role and be fulfilled while doing it.

Daddy — what a precious word to hear!

My Commitment to Fatherhood

Based upon what I have learned in this chapter, I will treasure the fact that my children are totally dependent upon me in the following ways:

1. _____

2. _____

3. _____

4. _____

5. _____

And I pledge to NOT let them down.

Keeping It Simple

By Veronica Grabill

The Beginning

I met Vic at a church event. Divorced for four years, he was the custodial parent of his seven-year-old daughter, Ashley. I was divorced and the mother of three children; LaKeisha was seventeen, Ryan was nine and Lauren was four years old.

During our months of dating, we selected activities that included our children. We rode bikes, hiked at John Bryan State Park and then stopped by Young's Dairy for milk shakes. Some days, we simply played on the swing set in the backyard. Vic and I agreed to include the children and develop their acceptance of our relationship.

As our relationship flourished, we decided to involve the children in planning our wedding. We invited close friends and relatives to an outdoor poolside ceremony. Our children were excited about joining our families together. My kids struggled to accept a new father and sister. With Ashley being an only child and living with her father, her adjustment to three new siblings and a stepmother was not easy. Ashley surprised me when she said, "Let's not say stepfamily." Years later, our kids refer to each other as sisters or brother and to Vic and me as their parents. Much to our amazement the children have blended well.

Inclusion

We felt it was vital for our children to feel a part of the dynamics of being in a new family. When we went house hunting, we focused on purchasing a home that provided all the children with their own bedrooms to personalize as they chose.

As the oldest child, LaKeisha had a lower-level room with a deck, which was a great place for a young lady to have her privacy. Her siblings had hopes of moving down there once she moved out on her own. Ryan, our athlete, had a soccer and basketball décor. Ashley wanted peacocks painted on her wall that we decorated with rich burgundy tones. Lauren chose teal and lavender with dragonflies to decorate her room. This ownership provided each child a place in the family and a sense of belonging.

Everyone had assigned chores including making the bed and being dressed for breakfast. This expectation worked amazingly well. The kids needed parameters and guidelines and the routine relieved a lot of morning stress for me.

We had family meetings on a regular basis. The gatherings gave everyone the opportunity to speak their mind. Anyone could call a meeting whenever they had something on their heart — be it a complaint, concern, or hurt feelings. This format enabled us to put everything on the table and avoid emotional eruptions from built-up anxiety.

As a bedtime ritual, the kids took turns having devotions in their room. Vic and I prayed with each child separately in each room prior to turning out the lights.

We committed to finding a church together. We wanted to get involved and worship as a family. We didn't want to go to his church or my church, so we set out to find a church together. We visited seven or eight churches before we found one that the family called home.

From the onset, we committed to attending the kids' school activities and sporting events as a family. The "you go to your child's event and I'll go to mine" philosophy was unacceptable.

Keeping It Simple

Vic and I talked about the benefits of sessions with a professional counselor. We discussed it as a family unit and then made an appointment with a Christian counselor. Each child shared his or her feelings about the divorce and remarriage in a non-threatening environment. The sessions with the unbiased person were priceless.

The product of a divorced family, I remember wondering why my parents split up and would they ever get back together. We wanted our family to have an outlet through professional help and to understand that they were not at fault for the failed marriages. They knew that Vic and I would do everything in our power and with the guidance of God Almighty to be committed to this marriage. The assurance put them at ease.

Vic carved out time with each child. The one-on-one interaction made them feel special. Every Saturday, he took a child for breakfast at a restaurant of their choice — just the two of them.

Visitation

All of the kids followed the same visitation schedule. They left on the same day and returned home around the same time. This technique worked for several reasons: no one felt left out or missed out on anything while they were at their other parent's house. It also gave Vic and me time to ourselves.

When the kids returned home, we did not drill them about activities. We did not want to make them feel guilty for having fun or loving the other parent. We gave them freedom to enjoy the time they had with the other parent. This rule helped to smooth the transition between homes. We did not criticize what they did with the other family. Nor did we try to out-do or compete by comparing events, vacations or shopping trips. We created an environment that was normal, loving and accepting. A stable home for the children.

To Do It Over Again...

I would read as much as possible on blended families and talk to others who have journeyed down this path. I would establish boundaries from the beginning. And pray, pray and pray some more. Seek God and search the Scriptures for guidance.

Meditate on the following verse:

Love is patient, love is kind, and is not jealous; love does not brag and is not arrogant, does not act unbecomingly; it does not seek its own, is not provoked, does not take into account wrong suffered, does not rejoice in unrighteousness, but rejoices with the truth; bears all things, believes all things, hopes all things, endures all things. Love never fails.
~ I Corinthians 13:4-7 (NIV)

Today's Happenings

I am happy to say that thirteen years later our marriage is solid. We have successfully raised our children to be responsible, outgoing, social individuals. They have spread their wings and ventured out into the world.

Reconnaissance Mission

By Rita Smith
Written by Valerie L. Coleman

After numerous failed attempts to arrange visitation, my husband's seven-year-old son and eight year-old daughter were dropped off at our front door, unannounced. With only a four-hour prior visit under our belts, their mother planned for them to stay with us a month. Years into our marriage, with two daughters and the third one on the way, his children barraged me with disrespect, rejection and blatant defiance.

When they came to visit, they marched into the house like militant soldiers. With army fatigues boasting "I was here first" across their chests, they dared me to knock the insignia off of their uniforms. They mounted an all-out assault on the enemy, and the enemy was me.

My presence represented the end of the possibility of reconciliation between their biological parents. Giving me any inkling that they liked or cared about me would be classified as espionage, or worse yet, treason against their mother. On one occasion, my husband's son challenged me.

"My dad is my dad. My mom is my mom. But who are you? You're just a stepmother." He laughed and walked away.

Frustrated with trying to win the affection of my husband's children, I took my heavy heart to the Lord. "Okay, Lord, what is it that You want me to do? Show me how to love someone that doesn't want me in the picture." Sprawled out on the bedroom floor, I sought the Lord until my voice was hoarse. "What is Your desire for me concerning these people in my life? I've got to accept them, so why I am fighting this so much? Help me to build a bond and get to common ground with them."

As I lay prostrate before the Lord, He said, "Hunger for their souls." I got up from the floor and called out to God for clarification. The more I prayed, the more He revealed to me. This struggle was not a test of my faith, but an opportunity to win souls for the Kingdom. With my hands raised, I paced and made my requests known.

"Oh God, I ask for Your forgiveness. Purify my heart and renew my spirit. Father, cover the atmosphere in their home and protect their environment so they can sleep and rest at night. I speak peace in their lives. Lord, keep them from the wrong crowd. Bless them in school and keep trouble away. Don't let them fall victim to peer pressure. Help them to understand the lesson plans. English, math, spelling, Father pour Your wisdom into them. Marinate the seed that is planted in them. Let it grow until they become hungry for You."

Then, without warning, He shifted my petition. "Lord, please mend their mother's heart, so she can draw closer to You. And as she seeks You, send Your angels to minister to her. I call for peace in her mind, body and soul. Bless her finances. Bring in money so that every need will be met. Let them want for nothing."

As I freshened up for dinner, the Lord spoke to me. "The next time she drops off the kids, lock onto her. Hug her and don't let go."

Keep in mind that our interaction up to this point had been volatile. At times, I felt like I had stepped on a land mine. Isolated, I stood alone in the field, waiting for someone to rescue me. I dare not lift my foot, breathe or say a word, for fear of the inevitable explosion. But God is faithful. Not only did He give me the assignment for their souls, He gave me peace to submit to His command. I understood that I had to be presentable, polite and respectable at all costs. Not for my husband, the kids, their mother or myself. I had to do this to show the love of Christ.

So about a week later, when she brought the kids for a visit, I met her at the door. As the kids ran into the house, I embraced her. "Oh God, I ask that You cover her with Your love. Mend her broken heart. I command confusion, anger and pain to leave." At first, she hesitated to respond, but as I prayed, her heart melted and she cried.

"Father, lift every burden. Be a light in her spirit, so she doesn't live in darkness. The enemy cannot bind her with the cares of the world. Protect her emotions. Settle rest on her body so she is not weary. Peace, follow her. Tranquility in the name of Jesus." I had been so consumed with my own pain, that I didn't realize she was hurting too.

The transition did not happen over night. Flesh came against me when I committed to their souls, but it was my job to show them Christ. I didn't have time to dwell on flesh. The more I interceded on their behalf, the more insight the Lord gave me. He showed me how to respond to their comments and how to interact with them. As my fervent prayers penetrated heaven, God developed a sincere desire within me for their salvation. He filled me with His agapé love and demanded that I pour that same love out on them. He mended my broken heart with concern for their welfare. I no longer saw them as flesh, but souls for His use. I put myself under subjection and let Him minister to their needs.

Today, our lives are a witness to God's grace and mercy. The children are loving and respectful. Their mother brings groceries, bakes cookies at my house and buys gifts for my biological children. She calls me daily for prayer and spiritual guidance. We have Bible study and speak words of encouragement and blessings over our homes and families. We ask the Lord to bless our children and help them understand their homework. We petition Him to talk to them in prayer and dreams, and expose them to any mischief they are causing in the homes.

Through our joint prayer and fellowship, the Lord gives her revelation into my life. She often calls to encourage me. "Rita, God is going to reward you for the commitment you have shown to Him. Thank you for being real about God and showing me Jesus. I love you and I thank God for you."

Needless to say, our relationship impacted our lives and the lives of those around us. Outsiders were, and still are, confounded. We have both been called crazy for our connection — an inseparable spiritual connection.

You cannot combat a spiritual enemy with carnal weapons, so invest in prayer like you would invest in stocks. If you remain consistent, in the long haul, you will reap a great return and win the spoils of war. Suited in camouflage fatigues, I went behind enemy lines, crept into his camp, and took by force what belonged to God. I thank the Lord for my extended family because they made me tap into unconditional love.

United We Stand

By Lisa Vaughn

And the two shall become one flesh.
~ Genesis 2:24

With a blended family, one or both spouses bring children from a previous relationship into the marriage. Oftentimes, this complicates the process of becoming one flesh.

> *Wherefore they are no more twain, but one flesh. What God has put together, let not man put asunder.*
> ~ Matthew 19:6

Many people read this Scripture and apply it only to adults. I believe that children are included too. My transition from single mother to wife and mother of more has afforded me the opportunity to share from personal experience. I've listed elements critical to the success of our blended family:

✝ Before you say, "I do,"
  - Make an agreement to stand united. God honors marriage, so the husband and wife must commit to making the relationship a priority. Once the children are grown and gone, where will the marriage stand?
  - Understand your mate's beliefs on discipline and parenting. Is your mate a strict disciplinarian or laid back? When it comes to the rod of correction, the biological parent should administer the punishment.
  - Establish expectations for the children. The Bible refers to the family structure with the husband as the head, then the wife, then the children. Everyone needs

to understand their God-ordained order in the family. Expectations need to be communicated relative to homework, chores, curfews and privileges. The couple also needs to develop expected behavior outside the home, whether with the non-custodial parent or grandparents.

o Determine an appropriate name/title for the new parent. An older child may be reluctant to refer to the new husband as Daddy, without first establishing a relationship. Forcing the issue may cause more harm than good.

✟ The husband and wife must always convey unity and support for one another and present decisions as we and not I. Children should never see division in your relationship, decision-making or discipline. Settle disagreements away from the children.

✟ Have weekly meetings and family prayer. These sessions allow the children to openly express their feelings in a comfortable environment. This gathering is a great time to reiterate the house rules and make adjustments as the children mature. The family can set goals relative to growing the relationship, vacations, etc.

✟ Be aware that children may attempt to cause division in the marriage by involving the other parent, grandparents and siblings. If the children do not agree with the stepparent, they may express their frustration to someone outside the home. Oftentimes, the outsider gets an exaggerated story and may try to intervene causing more frustration for the marriage and ultimately the family.

Peace Be Still
By Carolyn Carnegie

At the onset of our union, we did not know Jesus as our Savior. But now, after eighteen years of marriage, I realize that the Lord crafted our blended family from the start.

The majority of our challenges dealt with parenting. I entered the marriage with a ten-year-old son. James, my husband, had a six-year-old daughter and a son twice her age. Before the divorce was final, Jim's ex-wife moved their children to another state. Their departure left a void the size of Grand Canyon in his heart and it wasn't long before his hurt manifested.

"Carolyn, why are you babying him?"

"I'm not babying him," I said with my hands on my hips. "He's not old enough to cut the grass. He could hurt himself on that mower."

"You need to wean him and cut the apron strings." He stomped out the back door. "He's never going to be a man with you pampering him."

"Whatever," I yelled through the kitchen window.

"Momma's boy." He cranked the mower and masked my expletives. Wounded.

We slapped some gauze on the problem. Before the cut healed, we had another encounter. Slap. The next tug-of-war left a gash three fingers wide. Slap. Our first year of marriage was like trying to cover a severed artery with a band-aid.

"Momma, I don't think Jim likes me."

"What do you mean? He loves you." I sat on the couch and rubbed my baby boy's back.

"He's way too strict." He dropped his head and mumbled, "And he complains that I don't do enough around the house."

"Well, you could keep your room clean."

"See, you always take his side."

"I'm not taking his side." I sighed. "Okay, I'll talk to him." A few days later, I mustered up the nerve to express my concern for his stern discipline.

"You've spoiled him rotten," James said, as we set the dinner table.

"Here we go again."

"Well you have. You need to let me work with him. He's going to grow up to be a sissy."

"No he's not." I shrugged and placed the basket of rolls on the table. "I think it's your approach. You intimidate him with your confrontational discipline. I'd appreciate it if you would ease up on him."

"Ease up? He needs to grow up, and you're talking about easing up." He chuckled. "You've got to be kidding."

"No, I'm very serious. I want you to give him some slack. You're too hard on him."

"You keep undermining my authority. It's like you're intentionally trying to keep us at each other."

"That's not true. I —" My son walked into the kitchen. "How about we save this conversation for later."

"Yeah." A plate clanked to the table. "Don't forget my kids are coming next week."

"I know."

"It's been almost a year since I've seen them. I'm really looking forward to their visit."

"Yeah, me too." We settled into a quiet meal and tension lingered in the air. As the night progressed, my emotions flooded me. I sat in the bathroom and cried.

~ ~ ~ ~ ~ ~ ~

Jim drove to North Carolina to bring the kids back to Dayton for a two-week stint. From the beginning, we encountered resistance from his son. With his daughter only seven years old, her rebellion manifested years later.

"Hey kids, this is my wife, Carolyn," Jim said, as he put their luggage in the guest room.

"Hi, Carolyn," his sweet daughter said. Junior walked past me without speaking. I looked at James and shrugged.

"Don't worry, honey. He'll come around."

No matter what I tried, Junior was not receptive to me. He seemed to be programmed to cause trouble.

"Why did you break my shelf?" I asked Junior.

"Because."

"Because is not an answer, young man." I took a deep breath to calm myself. "Now you need to explain to me why you broke my shelf."

"Because my mother told me to," he ran out of the living room.

"I don't believe this." I sat on the couch and looked at the mess on the floor. I picked up the remnants of my shelf and knick knacks and threw them away. No sense getting Junior in trouble with James. They'd be going home soon.

While we were at work during the day, the kids stayed home. Junior took this time to taunt my son. Although Junior was only a few inches taller than my son, he bullied him all day. He pushed and shoved him, called him names and even hit him on occasion.

Having been an only child, my son had no experience with sibling rivalry. Every day for a week, my baby boy pleaded for me to stay home. Since I did not have the luxury of taking time off work and for fear of his safety, I caved and took him to my mother's house. Jim did not approve.

"You're making a big mistake Carolyn. You're smothering that boy."

"Well if you don't like it, why not make Junior behave? He's instigating all this confusion and you're not doing anything about it."

"He's just being a boy. That's what they do, play rough."

"Well, I don't like the way he plays, and I'm not subjecting my son to any more of his boyish games."

"I still say that you're making a mistake."

"I'm trying to raise him to the best of my ability." Tears formed in my eyes.

"Your best just ain't good enough."

I exited the room and ran to the bathroom. Let the tears flow.

~ ~ ~ ~ ~ ~ ~

By the time the kids went back to North Carolina, I was spent. Instead of working together to resolve our differences in parenting, I conceded to James. I lost myself trying to please him and grew more frustrated.

"You love your son more than you love me," my husband said.

"No I don't, honey. Where is this coming from?"

"Just admit it."

"There's nothing to admit. I love you both, but in different ways."

"Yeah, right." He stormed out of the house and I went back to my crying room.

A couple of years into the marriage, we had a daughter. Three years later, we had a son. Yours, mine and ours. By the time our son was born, his daughter was on the let's-make-Daddy-and-Carolyn-miserable kick too. She made a long-distance call to the house. "Is my daddy there?"

"No, honey he isn't. Would you like to leave —" Click. "No she didn't just hang up on me." When I spoke with my husband about his daughter's disrespectful telephone etiquette, he brushed it off. Pummeled by accusations, disrespect and threats, I excused myself to the water closet.

~ ~ ~ ~ ~ ~ ~

We were pulled from both directions. While I experienced heartache from my husband's kids, an on-going fight had ensued between James and my son. I was the referee, but didn't know the rules of the game. The title bout went on for years, even after we gave our lives to Christ. As a matter of fact, after we got saved, the enemy's flood gates opened and chaos erupted in our home. Devastated, consumed and tired of trying, the pressure almost broke me. We were in the midst of spiritual warfare.

As a babe in Christ, I did not know a lot about the Word. I did know that this battle was the Lord's and I had to give it to Him. I converted the bathroom into my throne room and spent time in my Daddy's face. I sought Him for wisdom and understanding. I wanted to handle myself in a way pleasing to Him. I needed to usher in peace and set the atmosphere of praise in my home.

I now understand that God carried us through the most difficult times. If not for His grace and mercy, I would have walked, or better yet, run out of this marriage. The following Scriptures helped me stay focused as we were tossed in the storm:

> *For the battle is the Lord's and He will give you into our hands.*
> ~ I Samuel 17:47b

Trust in the Lord with all your heart; and lean not to your own understanding. In all your ways acknowledge Him, and He will direct your paths.
~ Proverbs 3:4–5

Finally, my brethren, be strong in the Lord, and in the power of His might. Put on the whole armor of God that you may be able to stand against the wiles of the devil. For we wrestle not against flesh and blood, but against principalities, against powers, against the rulers of the darkness of this world, against spiritual wickedness in high places. Wherefore take unto you the whole armor of God that you may be able to withstand in the evil day, and having done all, to stand.
~ Ephesians 6:10–13

When God puts a blended couple together, it is advantageous to discuss rules of the home, discipline, finances and other important issues that will impact your household.

Remember that the enemy hates families, and he will do all he can to keep us divided. That's his job. However, as parents of blended families, we must learn to stay two steps ahead of the enemy by seeking God for direction, praying for each other (James 5:16) and praying together. We ignite God's power when we touch and agree (Matthew 18:19–20). Don't allow yourself to be overcome with fear. Your situation is not hopeless. God has given us power over the enemy (Luke 10:19). We just need to use it.

We serve an awesome and powerful God. He longs to see us victorious in every area of our lives. And after years of praying and seeking Him, my husband and biological son now have a wonderful relationship. I pray that you let God take you through whatever storms arise in your family, just like He took us through ours. We continue to seek Him, and we have been honored to have God calm the raging seas in our lives.

Peace be still!

Covenant Keepers

By Craig Coleman, Sr.

In Genesis, chapters 15 to 25, we see the blended family dynamics of Abram, Sarai and Hagar. Imagine living in the same home with your spouse, your ex and the child that you and your ex bore together. For thirteen years, Sarai had to watch her husband and his mistress raise a child together. What kind of drama do you think they had in their home?

The connection that you have with your children is linked to the bloodline that cannot be broken. No matter what type of relationship you have with your biological children, they will always be your children. But the relationship you share with your spouse is a covenant made to God. I have found that a promise or covenant can be broken without much effort, but the bloodline that ties us to our children is not as easily severed. Therefore, the process of becoming one flesh takes a considerable amount of effort, especially in a blended family. Below is a summary of observations and situations that had the greatest impact on our struggle for oneness.

<u>Time Invested</u>

Because we lived under the same roof, developing a relationship with Valerie's biological children came easy. The time invested did not require special effort because we saw each other every day. However, the time that my wife invested with my birth children was mainly during visitation. This discrepancy definitely had an impact on the relationship between my wife and kids.

On The Road

Vacationing was a problem that popped up from time to time. We planned a family trip to Gatlinburg, Tennessee in a mountaintop chalet. To get the whole family there, we were going to rent a passenger van. I called my ex and told her that we would take care of everything — food, transportation, and lodging — but needed her to send the kids with spending money. For the four-day trip, we figured they would need about fifty dollars each. My ex said that the money issue was our problem. "So if you can't pay for everything, then they don't go." We cancelled the van reservation and drove our five-seater to Dollywood.

Pushed And Broken

My wife and biological son have always had a good relationship. But when it came to my daughter, Valerie had to go the extra mile. Her friend, Vanessa Miller, had won a trip to Gatlinburg and invited Valerie to attend. Vanessa was taking her daughter and asked Val to bring someone to keep her company. At her friend's request, Valerie invited my daughter. With meals and lodging covered, we agreed to pick up any other expenses my daughter may have required. They confirmed the trip about four months out and finalized the arrangements.

Three days before their scheduled departure, my daughter cancelled. She said that she would be out of town visiting family members. Disappointed, Valerie contacted our niece, Tamiracle, and she jumped on the opportunity. On Saturday afternoon, I called the ex's house to check on my son. My daughter answered the phone.

"I thought you were out of town this weekend."

"I'm sorry that I lied, Daddy. But if I start getting along with your wife, I will be stabbing my mother in the back."

At this point, my wife was broken. The relationship that she tried to build became even more difficult. A vacation opportunity has not been offered again.

Leave, Cleave and Weave

My most difficult struggle. My wife and I understood what it meant to leave your parents, cleave to one another and weave into one flesh (Ephesians 5:31). We knew that we were supposed to honor and place each other second only to Christ. Whether parents, children or siblings, we understood our place. But the relationships with our biological children soon changed that philosophy.

~ ~ *The Odd Man Out*

I had a great relationship with Valerie's sons. I attribute a large portion of our success to us residing in the same house. But situations arose that made me question if I was number one in her life. My wife could be watching television or doing something pertaining to her job or business. If I attempted to start a conversation, she would ask me if I could wait until she finished. I honored her wishes and let her finish without interruption. However, if one of the boys approached her, no matter what the situation, she took a break and gave them her undivided attention.

Being one to avoid conflict, and with all the other chaos we had in our lives, I chose not to fight this battle. When I finally mentioned it to Valerie, it was no longer an issue. The boys were grown and had left for college. Over the years, I noticed that Valerie attended to the needs of all children in that manner — nieces, nephews, God kids and neighborhood kids. And since making her aware of my concern, she's been more attentive to me.

~ ~ *Daddy's Number One Girl*

My daughter and I had a relationship that differed from my other children. Because she was the only girl, I found myself defending and putting her ahead of my wife. Nothing I planned, I just did not believe that I favored my daughter. However, Valerie felt differently and did not have a problem bringing this to my attention.

Since my daughter was not happy with my decision to remarry, she chose not to get along with my wife and pursued every opportunity to stir up conflict. One weekend, a situation opened my eyes. My wife was washing dishes in the kitchen as my daughter and I carried on a conversation. Out of nowhere, my daughter asked a question that I did not know how to answer. "Daddy, am I your number one girl?"

I said what came to mind. "Yes baby. You know that you are my number one girl and Valerie is my number one lady." That statement made my daughter feel good, but as I attempted to kiss my queen, her actions showed me that I messed up in the worst way. When I took the kids home, I explained to my daughter that she and my wife were both number one, but in different ways.

"But Daddy, I thought that I was number one."

"You are my number one; my number one girl."

"But you said in the house that I was your number one."

I realized that my daughter meant number one female as opposed to my use of girl versus woman. "You are my number one girl. This is not a competition between you and my wife."

When I returned home, my wife informed me that I did not handle that situation well. She said that she was tired of me putting my daughter first all the time. She went on to say that I should have corrected my daughter on the spot in her presence, to reinforce our position as husband and wife. My daughter continued to challenge Valerie's position as wife and lady of the house.

Despite the adversity to reach a place of oneness, Valerie and I stood on God's Word.

> *For this reason, a man will leave his father and mother and be united to his wife, and the two will become one flesh. This is a profound mystery — but I am talking about Christ and the church.*
>
> ~ Ephesians 5:31–32 (NIV)

Although we are still juggling issues to bring balance to our blended family, the Lord continues to keep us.

His Number One Girl

By Valerie L. Coleman

The family had just finished Sunday dinner. I clanked dishes in the soapy water, while everyone else sat around the fireplace enjoying reruns of *The Cosby Show*. Ten minutes later, I joined the group in the family room.

"Daddy, aren't I your number one girl?" The hairs on my neck stood at attention. Our blended family consists of four boys and one girl. Our thirteen-year-old daughter, my husband's oldest biological child, jockeyed for her position on a regular basis. I cocked my head to the left and with my eyes fixed on his mouth, waited for his reply.

"Baby, you're daddy's number one girl," he said as he stroked her hand. My upper lip curled. "But Valerie is my number one lady." He caressed my back and smiled. My contorted face relaxed a smidgen. The opportunity to affirm me presented itself and he wimped out. Later that evening, I expressed my contempt.

"Babe, why did you tell her that she was your number one girl?"

"Because she is my number one girl," he said as he slapped some Colgate on his toothbrush.

"I know, but her motive for asking was to force you to choose between me and her." I slipped on my pajamas, stomped into the bedroom and plopped on the bed. "Why didn't you correct her?"

"I didn't see a need to correct her. She didn't do anything wrong."

"See, that's what I'm talking about. You miss all the subtle things she says or does to get under my skin."

"So why do you keep exposing yourself?"

"Good night, Craig." I snatched the covers and rolled over. No kisses tonight.

In preparation for this blended family anthology, I interviewed Brenda McKinney, a licensed social worker and family therapist. I shared the event with her. "Can you believe that? His number one lady," I said, with my head shifting from side to side. "What a cop out."

"Actually, your husband gave the best possible reply."

"Really? How's that?" Curious George walked into the room and jumped on my back.

"His response validated both of you. He acknowledged her position as daughter and yours as wife. He put a stop to the game without creating chaos. I'm really quite impressed."

"Wow. I wish I had known that seven years ago."

Consumed with the princess' attempt to dethrone me, I failed to realize that my queendom was never in jeopardy. She believed that if she lost her place as daddy's number one girl, then she would also lose his love. Her statement was not an attack against me, but a call for reassurance that their relationship was still solid.

So after eating a full-course meal of shame salad, meathead meatloaf, stir-fried stupid, topped off with humble pie for dessert, I apologized to my husband. Kisses tonight.

A Threefold Cord Is Not Easily Broken

By Wendy E. Hayes

My husband and I have been together for fourteen years including our three-year courtship. During that time, my relationship with our baby's mama has matured to a level of love that most find difficult to understand. We are friends; however it did not start off that way. She and I were enemies; at least I believed she viewed me as such. But now, through the grace of God, we are friends with one goal: to raise our children to be God-fearing, intelligent, caring, tolerant, loving and compassionate individuals.

One might ask, "How can it get to this point?"

- First of all, all hidden agendas must be exposed. Everything has to be put on the table. Who actually initiates the exposition does not matter — the point is that it occurs. It will be painful and can get very ugly, but it must happen; the sooner the better. In my case, I demanded that we all sit and talk it out before the wedding.

- The male involved must be totally honest and firm about his feelings and intent with everyone concerned. Information is power. If he truly loves you, he should be willing to express his intentions. If you don't like what is revealed, at least you have the opportunity to abandon the ship before it sails. Don't fool yourself. If things are happening now (e.g. exchanging gifts, meeting for lunch and dinner) without your knowledge, it will continue. You need to know exactly where you stand. Believe me, she will be all too happy to let you know what has been going on behind your back, if her motive is to bring an end to your relationship.

- His concentration must be on you and his children — period. If he is trying to appease his ex, you have a problem. He cannot fall prey to manipulation (such as withholding visitation, etc.). You cannot compete with his children, nor should you be made to feel like you do. We are dealing with two different types of love. Make sure the two of you know the difference. He cannot and will not make everyone happy in this situation.

- You and your mate must be strong enough to take a stand. He has to make the ex and their children respect you and your relationship/marriage or you will be miserable until he does. Determine how tolerant you are willing to be and then adhere to it.

- Lastly, family and friends are an important component in the maturing process. Stay away from those who encourage you to be overly suspicious. Instead, use the good sense with which God blessed you. If it smells like a dog, walks like one and acts like one — well, you know the rest. This endeavor is not for the faint or jealous hearted. You have to be strong and confident in yourself to make a family out of these pieces. Your baby's mama is and should be a part of your family because like it or not, she is a part of his.

The bottom line is God can change any situation. If you, your spouse and the other parent truly want what is best for the children, then you will all put your personal hang-ups aside and focus on developing respectful relationships. Your behavior toward each other will contribute more toward the children's development into respectful, unselfish and loving individuals than any outside influence.

Before You Begin

By Joy Lewis

Growing up in a single-parent household was the least of Elizabeth's concerns. Paramount on her mind was fitting in at the new middle school, until her mother got married half way into her first year. Without any consideration of the pre-teen's feelings, her mother announced that she had eloped to Las Vegas.

The stranger moved into her house and invaded their privacy. He even had the nerve to bring a daughter with him. Who was he? Elizabeth set out to know and pretended to let down her guard. He appeared to be a nice guy, but the tinge that gnawed at Elizabeth told her different. He soon validated her suspicions.

He came home all hours of the morning and clanked open the garage door. Minutes later, he picked a fight with Elizabeth's mother. The verbal confrontations often ended in physical attacks. Every night Elizabeth begged her mother not to argue with him. She prayed that the stranger would not hit her and some nights it worked. Instead of beating her mother, he broke something in the house.

~ ~ ~ ~ ~ ~ ~

Some parents get so caught up in finding and keeping a mate that they forget about their children. Marriage is a huge decision, and the impact is exponential when blending a family. This life-changing decision must not be taken lightly. Some problems can be avoided if the single parent includes the children in the decision-making process. Children are affected too. Don't assume they'll deal with it, until they are old enough to move out.

Have you ever stopped to ask your children how they feel? Granted, some children may be too young to voice their opinion, but actions speak volumes. Don't count out their voices. Encourage plenty of gathering time before the relationship is consummated in marriage.

The Check for $3.96

By Sonya Visor

Grappled with the pending uncertainty, my leg shook under the table. In a few minutes, the court would decide which child would eat this week: our one-year-old son or my husband's eleven-year-old son from a previous relationship. We waited as the magistrate left the courtroom to formulate his decision. Who would be first on the list?

The magistrate returned with the ruling — his oldest son will eat this week. At the final strike of the gavel, they left us with a check for $3.96. How were we going to make it? Who was going to provide for my son?

My husband had just started a new job and was out ill for three days the previous week. You guessed it; no sick time. So after taxes, insurance and the child support payment, we had a whopping $3.96 left for the son I birthed. The court decided for me who was first. Responsibility of provision was made for one son, but not the other.

I stared at the check with my mouth gaped open. I looked at my husband, then back at the check. Fear gripped me as I contemplated how we would make it until his next paycheck. My hands trembled without restraint. My leg shook with so much force that I banged my knee on the table.

A flood of emotions bombarded me. Foolish for getting into this predicament. Angry that an outsider dictated how our money would be spent. Hurt that my son would go without milk and diapers. Then nobility stepped in, but only for a moment. Because when I looked at my child, I knew that it wasn't fair to rob him — to rob us of our weekly groceries. I knew that paying support was the right thing to do, but what consideration was made for Junior?

My husband of almost three years stood without saying a word. His wide-eyed gaze and hunched shoulders spoke volumes. A responsible man and father, the frustration overwhelmed him. He fell into the chair and ran his hands through his hair. He provided for one child that week, but they both depended on him. He looked up at me with fear in his eyes and then dropped his head. While he dealt with his issues, I had to deal with mine — trying not to hurt anyone.

After a while, I did what any daughter would do, I called my mother. That's right; I called Mom and told her all about it. She listened to me and allowed me to vent. Even in my volatile emotional state, I didn't want to share with my husband. I knew that my words would cause him more hurt and only serve to beat him down. He didn't need or deserve the soured fruit of my lips. Was I trying to act like Mary Poppins? Of course not, remember I called my mother, sisters and my best girlfriend. I found out that my response was typical. Our tight budget was based on a little more than $3.96. We needed that money. God allowed me the time to be angry without sin, but He did not allow me to stay there and wallow in it.

I had a choice to make — resent the older son for the rest of my marriage or allow God to take full control of the situation. I didn't want to hold a grudge against the child. Nor did I want to be responsible for driving a wedge between my husband and his son. His son was here to stay. My marriage was solid, and I wanted to keep it that way. So, I chose life. I changed my mind — it changed my actions.

How did I make the best of the situation? I prayed. I had to. I needed assurance. Reminded that someone outside of our relationship required my husband's time and attention, required that I knew beyond any doubt he loved me. But to then be robbed of a week's budget is another story in itself. Now you are messing with my money. To even say "robbed" isn't fair, and I thank God that I've come a long way. I knew that my husband had a son before I said, "I do." I knew from the beginning that this man loved his son. If he didn't, I don't think I would have had anything to do with him.

The day I received the smallest payroll check in my life, I realized what kind of woman I was. I know women who have dealt with a lot of unnecessary drama and have become very bitter over it. I understand. But what I cannot justify is taking the frustration out on the children. In our case, the biological mother did not initiate the proceedings, so I could not fault her for the cash flow chaos either.

So after a couple of hours of pouting with my girls, I moved on. By doing so, the Lord provided for us and we didn't miss a step. My mother purchased diapers and formula and my sister brought over a bag of groceries. We also received a check in the mail. I made a decision to not harbor any resentment against the young man. He didn't get to pick his parents or his situation. I chose to marry my husband, and I accepted the package deal. I loved past the hurt. My husband and I both found out that love is an action word full of power. He pulled from my reaction knowing that we would make it through this transition. This hearing marked the beginning of building a bridge for us to walk across one plank at a time.

One day I'll have to tell you about the time I told my stepson that I didn't care if he liked me or not. But until then — follow your heart. Operate in total surrender to God knowing that He is bigger than anything you can ever go through. Peace unto you.

A Gentlemen's Agreement
The Unspoken Pact

By Wade Harper

Two men of different languages can communicate better than a man and a woman that speak the same language.
~ Author Unknown

I remember the anger that festered inside me when my not-so-stable life took a nosedive. Why did my life have to change because some guy wanted to get busy with my mom? Why my mother? He wooed and courted her like I was not in the room. If I weren't five years old, I would have reached up and slapped him.

After a few visits, the urge to slap Larry decreased. He acknowledged my presence and threw an occasional bone. His motive, although apparent to me, fell below my mother's radar. He did not use the get-in-good-with-the-kid-to-get-with-the-mother tactic. His motives were clear enough that a child could understand and I did.

Mama and Larry had a whirlwind courtship. During their yearlong fling, I resided with my maternal grandparents. Close to home, but out of the way. With the exception of a few outings, I spent little time with the happy couple. We made an effort to enjoy our time together, but I was definitely a third wheel.

After the wedding, our first year as a blended family was tough. Larry and I had a couple of clashes. Mama tried to grant Larry space to establish his role as man of the house. However, her protective instinct overruled many of his decrees. On one occasion, she supported her husband and did not interfere. Without her maternal influence, I had to pull out the big guns, Grandmamma and Granddaddy. After my grandparents unleashed their fury, a resolution was made. We formulated the gentlemen's agreement. I would be respectful of Larry and his place. In return, Larry would respect my personal space: my room, my safe haven. If necessary, I could retreat without fear of retaliation. As long as I kept my room clean and orderly, no one walked in or followed me in without my permission. The peace treaty had been established. Polite indifference, however, we mistook apathy for respect.

Eighteen months later, I had a baby brother. Not much of a surprise, since Mama and Larry mated like rabbits. They didn't watch television or read books. They kissed, cuddled and told me to stay out of the room when the door was closed.

Tony was a miniature version of his father. With his round face and wide nose, it seemed like Larry reproduced himself from a remnant sample. My rank reduced from first son to last loved. They gave birth to little Robinson Crusoe and I became Friday. Almost voted off the island, I obeyed their every command. I never volunteered to be the baby butler. Bottles. Diapers. Bibs. Clothes. The peace treaty had been breeched. War!

Over the next five years, the arguments escalated. Along with problems common to marriages in general, the blending process had taken its toll on the family. Larry made one last-ditch effort to keep the family together. His proposal: get me out of the house. Send me to my grandparents, military school or a boarding school. With me out of the picture, he could better provide for his family. One less mouth to feed and a lot fewer headaches.

"Look, Ida. I've really tried to make this marriage work," he glared at me and then continued. "But your son keeps stirring up mess."

"Larry, I don't care how much mess Wade creates, I am not shipping my son off to some military school. And my folks are too old to chase after him."

"Money is tight. I figured we could do better for the family if we sent him away."

"Think again." Mama stomped to the kitchen. I followed behind her.

"Mama, it's okay. I like the idea of staying with Grandma. I'm a big boy now. I can help around the house."

She leaned over to meet my gaze. "I know that you're a big boy, but you are not going to live with Grandma. I'm your mother and I will take care of you." She stood to confront Larry who had sauntered into the room.

"I have two sons, Larry. I thought you felt the same." She wiped the tear that danced down her cheek. "My family includes all of us; not just me, you and Tony."

"I didn't mean any harm. I was just trying to look out for us."

"Oh really? Keep looking."

"Mama, I want to go live with Grandma." I stood between her and Larry. "I don't like it here. I don't like him. I don't like that kid. And I don't like you."

Mama's face sank to the floor. Tears welled in her eyes and then trickled down her face. A couple of them splashed onto my cheeks. I turned to Larry. He appeared to be content with my defiance. His eyes hypnotized me to continue. I turned back to Mama.

"If you'll be happier without me around, then I'll leave. I just —"

"Don't ever say that again." She picked me up and gave me a bear hug. "Not having you here will only make me sad."

A few more occurrences of late-night brawls and I posed my offer again. Mama flashed the keep-talking-and-I-will-slap-the-taste-out-of-your-mouth look.

Divorce was inevitable. With Larry gone, Mama, Tony and I struggled for a long time. Mama went hungry many nights, so that Tony and I could eat. Larry had other kids and occasionally picked up Tony to spend time with his siblings. He returned home with a fresh hair cut, full belly and new clothes. The rejection consumed me. Mama called Larry.

"I appreciate what you're doing for Tony, but can't you do a little something for Wade too? His birthday is in a couple of weeks. How about you show him that you care and get him a few things?"

I couldn't believe all the gifts Larry bought for me. Big packages and small boxes, most of them wrapped in shiny paper. I ripped through several of them. Shoes. Socks. A couple of toys. Elated, I reached for one of the larger boxes.

"Oh, hold on Wade. That one is for Tony." Larry pulled the gift toward himself.

"Huh? It's not his birthday."

"I know, but I got him a few things too." He sorted through the remaining boxes, separating the gifts for his son and me, the bastard child. A few things ended up being half of the gifts.

Throughout the balance of our childhood, Mama stood like a flint. She gave Tony and me the greatest gift any parent could give a child. We witnessed her acceptance of Jesus. We watched her baptism. We observed her living for Him.

Now in my thirties, I see Larry on occasion. He lives alone and physical afflictions limit his mobility. Mama looks after him. Initially, apprehension soured in my mouth. I didn't understand how she could forget the past. How was she able to forgive?

But now that I have accepted the Lord Jesus for myself, I understand that real love does not hold a grudge. If you want to be loved, love as illustrated in I Corinthians 13. I have forgiven Larry and apologized to him for my actions. Not one of us set out to harm the other. We were not weapons of destruction, but instruments that God used to enrich and mature one another.

The institution of marriage and rearing a Christian family is difficult. And when the dynamics of blending families are added the situation is more complicated. In traditional families, the bond of kinship brings natural strength and cohesion. In blended families, the possibility exists that these bonds never form. However, in Christ, we are one family. His love transcends biological kinship. He will teach a father how to love all the children in his house. He will order our steps and guide our actions. Without this spiritual foundation, our blended family failed. I believe in my heart that had I known Jesus as my personal Savior and Larry had been a God-fearing man, our family may have overcome the odds.

The Daddy of Them All

By Idrissa Uqdah

When I was two years old, my mother married "The Daddy of Them All," his self-appointed moniker. A widower, he had an eleven-year-old daughter. My mother left her second marriage with my nine-year-old sister and me. For her, the third husband, a neighbor and friend of my mother's uncle, was a charm.

As the little darling, Daddy spoiled me rotten. They nicknamed me Daddy's PJ — his pride and joy. The following year, my brother was born. Two years later, I had another sister. When I was ten years old, the doctors diagnosed my mother with a tumor. Months later, the alleged abnormality turned out to be our baby sister.

We lived in a little row house in North Philadelphia, purchased with Daddy's veteran's benefits. He worked long, hard hours as a tool forger in the steel mills. My mother was charged with the responsibility of staying home to take care of the kids. Although she really wanted to work outside the home, Momma prepared a hot breakfast every morning before school. At lunchtime, we came home to food set on the kitchen table. Mother ironed clothes and watched *As The World Turns* while we ate lunch — usually soup, sandwich and fruit. Before we returned to school, she made sure our clothes were spotless. If not, we changed into fresh, clean attire. She either walked us to school or designated one of the older girls to make sure we got to school safe. We ate dinner at the dining room table at 5:00 p.m., when Daddy came home from work. Anyone absent from the table at chow time had to answer to Daddy. Our inner-city,

African-American family paralleled the Cleavers of *Leave It To Beaver.*

Our family life centered on a basic belief in God, the Bible and Daddy's rules. We attended various churches. Born in the Baptist tradition, Momma embraced the teachings of the Jehovah's Witnesses, until I was a teenager. Daddy remained a non-practicing Catholic, but respected my mother's religious choices for us.

They seldom went anywhere they could not take us, so we created a lot of fond memories and family traditions. Picnics at Fairmont Park and walks to the Philadelphia Zoo were great experiences. We went to the drive-in movies in Daddy's big old raggedy Buick and Chinatown for dinner once a week. I loved the times at Pat's Steaks in South Philadelphia. We hung out of the back window of the car and ate cheese steaks. Daddy stood outside and told funny jokes. We also had summer neighborhood block parties full of food, folks and fun. Music filled the air as we danced and sang.

Everyone was equal in our household. No one got special treatment. No his, hers and ours. We were not allowed to use the terms stepmother, stepfather, or step anything.

"Steps are what you walk up. I am the Daddy of Them All." My father's words resonated throughout our spirits for our entire childhood. He allowed no differences between us. He was Daddy. She was Momma. All of us belonged to both of them and they loved us unconditionally.

"From the cradle to the grave, you will always love each other." Daddy was a wise man and insisted that we support and care for each other. This credo helped our blended family survive. We dare not draw lines in the sand based on biological ties.

Our peaceful co-existence was complemented by the fact that the biological fathers were absent. No custody battles, no child support fights and no visitation issues. No outside interference.

My oldest maternal sister and I met our biological fathers as we approached adulthood. My father explained that he never interfered in my childhood because he knew that I was being well taken care of and he did not want to cause any problems. Both of my fathers sat together at my high-school graduation and cheered me on as I delivered my class valedictorian address. My biological father remained in the background and helped finance my college education.

When Daddy passed away, my biological father and I formed a relationship that lasted until his death ten years ago. I indeed had the better of two worlds. My older sister did not fair as well. The same alcoholism that forced the end of her father's marriage to Momma caused him to drift apart from my sister.

Our blended family is unique in today's society. God's grace and mercy kept us together. My parents' faith strengthened our family and gave us a basis to love one another. Raised the old-fashioned way, our parents respected and loved one another and taught us by example. My parents were not partial. Six kids with distinct personalities; my parents allowed us to be who we were. They encouraged us, protected us and taught us how to get along.

Today, my siblings and I spend a lot of time together. We live in close proximity to one another and our children have a cousin-hood of love and shared experiences. At family gatherings, we tell them stories and share photos of our childhood and our upbringing. We raised them the same way that we were raised and now they are nurturing and training their children.

My Baby's Daddy

By Deborah Ogletree

The boys played video games in the TV room. They mimicked the roar of racecars, as they pounded on the hand controls. Baby Girl sat at the dining room table. The pedestal chair dwarfed her tiny frame. Her patent leather shoes dangled as she swung her legs back and forth in rhythm with her favorite song.

"Jesus loves me this I know," she sang in sweet refrain. Content with her box of crayons and favorite coloring book, she continued. I hummed with her, as I prepared dinner.

"Who is my daddy?"

I continued to slice tomatoes and onions for a salad and scurried to the sink to rinse dishes. I walked back to the stove to check the simmering vegetable medley. I stepped toward the cabinet to grab the potholder, when I felt her gaze penetrate my back and pierce my heart.

"Mommy, who is my daddy?" She put down her crayon.

Lord, why is she asking about her daddy now? I paced. A few weeks prior, my sons' father picked them up for a weekend visit. Their toddler sister greeted my ex-husband, as he entered the front door.

"Hi, Daddy."

"I am not your daddy," he said. His bitter tone and harsh words made my stomach quiver.

"Baby Girl, this is Mister. He's here to pick up your brothers." I patted my sweet daughter on the head, as I cut my eyes at him. "That was uncalled for," I whispered, as Baby Girl walked away.

"Nobody told you to take on this responsibility." He motioned for the boys to head outside. "You make sure she doesn't refer to me as her daddy again."

The sound of vegetables in bubbling water and my boys' laughter in the TV room faded. The amplified beating of my heart engulfed my senses. Warmth shrouded my body as tears rose in my eyes.

"Mommy!" I turned and looked down to see Baby Girl standing beside me. With her eyes filled with tears, she tugged on the hem of my apron. "Who is my daddy?"

For years, I imagined my perfect family. Married to my high school sweetheart, I planned to have two boys and two girls. A year into our marriage, our son was born. Five years later, we had another son. The second pregnancy thrust me into a medical crisis. My doctor urged me to not have any more children. I agreed to a surgical procedure to prevent future pregnancies. Seven years into our marriage, my husband and I divorced. At twenty-seven years old, my fairy tale life shot me into reality. A single mother with two sons.

By the time I reached the age of thirty-eight, I experienced symptoms of pregnancy. Nausea, fatigue, weight gain. My emotions rocked from one extreme to the other like a music conductor's metronome. The ambivalent feelings taunted me day and night. When I went shopping, I browsed in the infants and toddler section looking at clothes for little girls.

I waited for God to take away my maternal feelings for another child. Still single, I dated on occasion, but no romantic interest that would lead to marriage. In earnest, I prayed for His direction and peace. My footsteps were ordered into a children's service agency that arranged county adoptions. I discussed my intentions with my sons.

"Now just because I'm considering adopting a child, that doesn't mean that I will love you two any less."

"Aw, Mom, we know that," my oldest son said.

"You've got enough love for us and ten more kids," my youngest son interjected.

We laughed. "Let's not get carried away. I just want to make sure you understand that we'll have to make some changes."

"Will you still be able to make my high school events?"

"Of course."

"Then I'm game."

"Me too."

With the approval of my two most important men, I shared my plans with other family members, co-workers and saints. The reply was a unanimous, "Have you lost your mind?"

I continued to pray and seek the Lord. I needed assurance that I was moving in His purpose and not acting on selfish motives. With God, all things are possible. My age, marital status and financial standing were insignificant in His sight. God had a plan; not only for my life, but also for the child I was compelled to bring into our home.

The name, Baby Girl, echoed in my spirit, before I knew anything about my child. I endured a series of home studies, meetings and a background check. Shirley, our caseworker, practically lived with us as part of the evaluation process. More than fifteen years my junior, her fragrant personality made the home visits special. She and the boys hit it off on the first visit.

About nine months into the adoption procedure, I was allowed to select a child. The receptionist ushered me into a room that resembled a college library. Volumes of books had pictures of children in need of families. The demand far exceeded the supply, so the agency allowed me to select from several neighboring counties.

I glanced from page to page. With each adoring face, I questioned how our society could have so many children, of various ages and races, without a family. Where are the grandparents, aunts, uncles, cousins or other family members? How did they allow these children to be pictured in a book as if bearing a sign reading "WANTED parents and family needed?"

Lord, how do I select a child? I trusted God. I knew that my steps were ordered in this path. With so many children, my emotions overwhelmed me. Unable to focus and maintain my composure, I opted to try again later.

The agency sponsored weekly support meetings to assist adoptive parents. At one gathering, I glanced at children's photos sprawled on a table. When my gaze fell on a picture of a little girl, I stared at her soft face. At fifteen months old, her bright yellow polka dot dress illuminated the picture like the sun on a calm spring day. Her white shoes and ruffled socks contrasted with her ebony skin. Her sweet, innocent smile stole my heart. I raced to Shirley to find out if she still needed a family.

"Yes, Marie is available. She lives in a Caucasian foster home. Her birth mother delivered an undersized infant, then walked out of the hospital a couple of days later. She's very bubbly and loves to sing and chatter."

I named her Maria and brought her home. The classes and sessions did not prepare me for the adjustment. Some days were calm, but other days the gale-force wind blew the life out of me. *My God what have I done?* Resting in the knowledge that I walked in my purpose, I rooted myself. I would never desert my birth sons and I refused to abandon her. She was now my child.

"I don't know who your daddy is." I wiped my hands on the apron and caressed her cheek. "The other mommy didn't give us any information about your daddy or herself."

"Does God know who my daddy is?" She clutched my waist and we embraced.

"Baby Girl, God knows your daddy and He told me to tell you that He is your Father."

This conversation occurred fourteen years ago and now Baby Girl is about to enter college. I give God the highest praise because He has been so faithful. My daughter has her own relationship with her Daddy, Abba Father. He would not allow me to abort the calling. Not at all like I had planned, but against the odds, I was given my perfect family. My sons are doing well. My daughter is my godsend. I meditate on the plans God has for our lives and He is to be praised.

I revised a Psalm in dedication to my daughter about her Father, my baby's Daddy.

> *I will praise Thee; for my child was fearfully and wonderfully made: marvelous are Thy works and that my soul as her mother knoweth right well. Her substance was not hid from Thee when she was made in secret, and curiously wrought in the lowest parts of the earth. Thine eyes did see her substance, yet being imperfect: and in Thy book all her members were written, which in continuance were fashioned when as yet there was none of them. How precious also are Thy thoughts unto her O God! Father, how great is the sum of them.*
>
> ~ Psalm 139: 14-17 (revised)

The Invisible Mom
By Gwendolyn Cox

I don't know why I get so anxious when our home is blessed with a new child. I guess it's because I want the child to feel welcomed. It must be frightening to be moved from one stranger's home to another's. I cannot pretend to understand the flurry of emotions that must flood their senses. Anxious. Afraid. Overwhelmed. Frustrated. Concerned. Mad. Angry. Disappointed.

So to alleviate some anxiety, I bake a homemade pound cake close to the child's arrival time and let the sweet aroma permeate the house. The first memory the child has of his new home is the mouth-watering smell of cake — a happy smell, a happy memory.

In 1998, a caseworker from children's services brought a fourteen-year-old Black male to live with us. As I opened the door, my eyes fixated on the most beautiful, gentle eyes I had ever seen, like those of a doe. Had he been a girl, I would have nicknamed him Bambi.

"Hi, you must be Tavion. I'm Mrs. Banks. Please come in." His caseworker followed behind him. She gave me a folder with paperwork to sign, asked to see his room, sat for ten minutes, then left to take care of her "real" family. "What do you want to call me? Mom, Grandma or Mrs. Banks?"

"I don't know," he said.

"Fair enough. Think about it and let me know."

Tavion's father was incarcerated and his mother was deceased. He had twelve siblings, including three sets of twins, whom he missed. But most of all, Tavion loved his mother. He missed her with a hurt that kept his heart in a perpetual state of mourning. He was sad and angry — very angry.

~ ~ ~ ~ ~ ~ ~

Six months later, Tavion's academic performance was horrible. I spent more time at school than he did. The school secretary often called to let me know that he was absent. When I tracked him down, I found out that Tavion climbed in a window at his friend's house and relaxed over there on school days. How can you learn, if you're not in class? Sometimes, the school administrator called because Tavion had busted someone in the mouth. His uncle was a famous boxer and Tavion wanted to follow in his footsteps, so his classmates became his punching bags and sparring partners. Per school policy, he had to be removed from school grounds. So, I dropped everything and picked him up. Instead of pronouncing the next round of the match for his school suspension, over dinner I talked to him about using a name or title to address me.

"Tavion, call me something. I don't care what, but it hurts me when you never address me as anyone." I chomped on a spare rib. "So what are you going to call me?"

"I don't know. I'll think about it," he mumbled.

"What's there to think about? Just call me Mrs. Banks, but call me something."

~ ~ ~ ~ ~ ~ ~

Attending church was mandatory at our home. During the summer of 1999, Tavion met thirteen-year-old Nora, and the kindred souls were joined at the hip. I told Nora's mother her daughter was too young to date, but she insisted it was okay.

The phone rang. "Your daughter-in-law's got something to tell you," Nora's mother said, insinuating that our children were playing house.

"What's up Nora?"

"Mom, I'm pregnant."

"When and where did that happen?" I always kept a close eye on them when they were at my house in the hopes of never having this conversation.

"It happened when you took us to the movies," her voice cracked. "That's why we weren't there when you came to pick us up. We left and went somewhere else."

Silence lingered on the phone. She had gotten pregnant on my watch. "Let me speak to your mom." After a brief intermission, the conversation continued. "So Miss It's-okay-for-my-daughter-to-date, what's the plan now?"

"I think she should have an abortion."

"I agree. She's only thirteen and she needs to finish school." The box office reviews were in — abortion it will be. Oh, but God! He sent a messenger who ministered to Nora and let her know that it was not God's will that she murder her child. Shame bombarded me and settled on my shoulders. Forgive me Lord.

> *Many are the plans in a man's heart, but it is the Lord's purpose that prevails.*
> ~ Proverbs 19:21 (NIV)

~ ~ ~ ~ ~ ~ ~

It's a boy! Tavion, Jr.! I, Granny Banks, had a front row seat for the feature presentation. The baby debuted a bit lighter than expected. Actually, considerably lighter than expected — he looked white. Tavion and I stared at each other like we had seen a ghost.

Without my knowledge, he signed the birth certificate, which infuriated his caseworker. With the light hue contrasting his father's pigment like a nineteen-inch black and white TV contrasts with a sixty-inch plasma, I had doubts that he fathered the child. I encouraged the teen parents to have a paternity test — partially because of the color spectrum variant, but also because of the couple's aggression toward each other. Every time Tavion and Nora had a disagreement, they challenged the baby's paternity. The paternity test confirmed it; Tavion, you are the father. Thank God, we can put that argument to rest.

The magistrate overseeing Tavion's case had tired of Tavion's poor decisions and questioned our parenting skills. She said that we were poor foster parents, unable to control Tavion. The magistrate ordered our son to be moved to another home.

What tripped me out was that Tavion was angry with me. I warned him on numerous occasions that if he continued his negative behaviors the courts would remove him from our home. He ignited this drama and now he's mad at me. He was the one with chronic truancy. He was the one fighting. He was the one making straight F's. He was the one who was a father at sixteen. But he's mad at me because he has to leave home. Go figure. The night before his departure, we had another bout. Round fifteen.

"Who are you mad at, Tavion? You don't call me anything, so how can you be angry with somebody who is nobody?"

"I want all my baby's pictures!"

"What do you mean you want all the pictures of the baby?"

"I want all the pictures," he walked to his bedroom and then slammed the door.

"Whatever! Just give me my frames! You can take the pictures!" I removed the pictures from the frames I had purchased. Petty, but I was mad and hurt.

The next morning, the caseworker took Tavion. My husband held me as I drenched his shirt with tears. He was placed with a single, Black female —the beginning of the end. Tavion needed a two-parent household.

For the next six years, I followed Tavion's life through friends and family. He visited on occasion, needing money or a bus pass. He called sometimes and asked for a ride. I was more than happy to accommodate him, just as any parent would help a child.

Twice he needed a place to live and my parents, who considered themselves his grandparents, rented their property to him. Although he never graduated from high school, he promised to work a legitimate job and keep his rent current. A few months later, he relinquished the apartment to drug dealers. God, how could he do this to my parents, not once, but twice?

~ ~ ~ ~ ~ ~ ~

In May 2006, after a leave of absence, Tavion came over to the house. We talked a long time. The best and most comfortable conversation we've ever had. After about an hour, I brought up the age-old taboo subject. Some time ago, Nora's mom told me that Tavion thought I was trying to replace his mother, and he would never allow that. I wasn't trying to replace her. He could simply call me, Mrs. Banks. He called my husband "Dad." I just wanted to be called something. When he called my cell phone, he simply said, "Hi, this is Tavion." Never, "Hi, Mrs. Banks."

"Tavion, why don't you call me something? When you came here, you were fourteen, now you're —"

"Do we have to talk about this now?" He fidgeted in his seat.

"Why not now? It's been eight years. Why can't you just call me Mrs. Banks?"

He stood. "I need to get a drink of water." He never returned to continue the conversation. I got the message and went to my room to watch TV.

A month later, an unfamiliar number flashed in my cell phone caller ID.

"Hello?"

"Mom, this is Tavion."

Mom? "Hi baby, what's up?"

"Nora and I are having a party for Aisha today. If you're not busy, I'd like for you to come." Tavion and Nora had another child, a beautiful girl celebrating her third birthday.

"I'd love to come. Are you sure it's okay with Nora?" There had been some family drama involving Tavion, Jr. and children's services. I wasn't sure if Nora wanted me around.

"It doesn't matter what she thinks. You're my family and I'm inviting you."

Family? "Okay, but I need to talk to Nora, first." I called Nora and she assured me that I was welcomed.

That was a great day. After eight years (the number of new beginnings), Tavion called me Mom, not Mrs. Banks, but Mom. At the picnic, he introduced me as his mother and everyone knew him as my son. The words "foster" or "step" were never used.

I love Tavion unconditionally. After the court-ordered separation, the double fleecing of my parents and refusal to acknowledge me by a name for eight long years, I still loved him. I think he now realizes that I will never leave him or forsake him. He is my family. He is my son.

Money

By Joshua Johnson, CFP®, RFC

Trees are in full bloom, sprinkled with pink, white and green. Plants and flowers peep through the ground after a long, cold hibernation. Birds sing early in the morning. Oh, you have waited an eternity for this time. You glance at the beautiful diamond engagement ring perched on your finger. It reminds you of all the tasks that lie ahead.

The bridesmaids' dresses need to be completed. Your search for a good disc jockey is still underway. Should you go with the white, chocolate or maybe yellow cake? Has your fiancé ordered his tuxedo yet? What about the groomsmen and their suits? Are the invitations printed? The mailing is scheduled for next month. The list goes on and on and on. But wait. Have you forgotten one of the most important priorities on your list (at least I hope it's on your list)? What about the money, honey?

Oh yeah! What about the money? Much time is spent on planning a one-day event, but very little time is spent discussing an issue that will affect your marriage the rest of your lives. With so many marriages disrupted for money mishaps, you would expect it to be priority one. Money can make us happy, greedy, miserable and just plain crazy all in the same day. This issue needs to be discussed sometime after the first date, but long before the honeymoon. Life together will flow smoother when everyone is on the same page. The topic gives you so much to talk about — credit issues, bankruptcy, income taxes, salaries, child support, alimony, college funding, etc. So let's start talking.

The two of you have been dating for some time now. You have an idea of each other's lifestyle and spending preferences. But do you really know how much is actually on the paycheck? What are the income sources? Are they working full or part time? They may be living off of credit to impress you, however their bottom line numbers read broke — so disclosure of actual income is necessary.

Keep in mind that money, or the lack thereof, is one of the leading causes of divorce. As a result, lifestyle changes may be required depending upon your desired standard of living and the household income. As a blended family, financial matters have exponential impact, in large part due to the needs of the children. Their inclusion could mean a reduction in the lifestyle you've grown accustomed to, to help support the new family. Your spouse may also have a drop in income for child support and/or alimony. Their gross annual salary may be $50,000, but their take-home pay may be reduced substantially. Bankruptcy can also deduct from their gross income. So, it's not the gross income, but the net income that is most important.

As you can probably tell, it is imperative to discuss the total household income prior to embarking upon holy matrimony. This interaction will, for the most part, determine your family's affordable lifestyle. Will the two of you combine your incomes or will you keep them separate? As a rule of thumb, I advise couples to combine all household income and treat it as "ours." In many cases, one spouse brings home all, or a greater portion, of the income. I still recommend combining it into the family pot. All of the household expenses including mortgage, credit card debt, groceries and vacations will be paid from the family pot. By using this strategy, you can eliminate many heated discussions. I've seen too many couples try to keep things separate and generally, at least one person is unhappy. Time out for paying everything Dutch.

Another point of awareness is income taxes. Your taxes may be affected because the additional money could place you in a higher tax bracket. Which in turn, could reduce some of the deductions that you used to claim. At the same time, your tax situation could improve as a result of the exemptions, I mean children, that are now a part of your life. Adjust your withholdings from your employer to have the appropriate amount of taxes withheld. During tax preparation, you have the option of filing jointly or separately as a married couple. Compare the results of both filing options every year. Any given year, one or the other can give you more favorable results.

If you normally receive a tax refund, this may be withheld if your spouse has accrued debt for child support or bankruptcy. Complete the injured spouse form to minimize disruptions to your refund. Otherwise, the IRS will send a letter notifying you that your tax refund has been applied to your spouse's accrued debt. Once the money is applied, it cannot be reversed. Also, if dealing with a previous marriage, check the divorce decree to determine if the custodial and/or non-custodial children can be claimed on your tax forms or the ex's. Some couples have the option of claiming the children every other year.

Are you ready for your next challenge? It's time to pay those bills. Yes, they're still going to show up even with your new family. Now this juncture is where things can become sensitive. Who's going to pay them? In most cases, each person is bringing some debt to the new relationship — some more than others. Let's look at our options.

The preferred method of handling daily money management is for everything to come out of one pot. In other words, combine all income into one joint account with each person having full access to the account. When it is time to pay the expenses, use the money in the joint account.

At this point, allocations should be made for personal spending allowances or guilt-free money. If she wants to buy new shoes with her allowance, this should not create any controversy. If he wants to purchase a new tie, that will be his prerogative. The two of you will have to come into agreement on the amount of the allowance — a critical factor dependent upon the amount of household income and expenses. Many families have a saver and a spender. The allowance concept helps keep the spender from getting out of control and the saver from being a penny-pinching miser.

The couple must also decide who will oversee the accounts as the family's chief financial officer (CFO). The optimal approach is for one person to handle the daily management. Typically, one person is better in this area. Men, you may have to put your ego aside and let your wife manage the daily activities, if she is better at it than you. Regardless of who earns the most income, utilize the spouse who controls the money better. One exception may be based on time availability. If the most qualified CFO travels frequently or works excessive hours, the other spouse may be forced to take on this responsibility. Remember, money allocation decisions are determined jointly.

As mentioned earlier, oneness is the preferred method. Some couples, however, choose to keep their finances separate. They maintain separate checking accounts, pay their bills individually and keep their debt separate. This strategy can lead to other questions. For example, who will pay the common household expenses such as the mortgage, utilities and groceries? You may elect to split expenses, but then you have to decide whether to divide them 50/50 or prorate them based on income. One spouse may choose to handle all of the household expenses and allow the other spouse free reign with their own money.

Another issue that must be resolved is the amount of giving to your church. The expectations between spouses can vary greatly, so it is important that the two of you come to an agreement.

What about the children? Before we get started, I must emphasize one point. When a man and woman decide to marry and they have children from previous relationships, the couple must agree on how money will be handled with respect to the children. This discussion and subsequent agreement must occur prior to marriage.

Now, let's talk about child support. As a stepparent, I have no idea what child support is. I have been involved in my son's life since he was three years old, and for the last seventeen years, we have never received a dime from his biological father. When his mother and I married, I felt responsible for his welfare as if he were my birth son. In other words, I provided shelter, clothing, food, school supplies, entertainment and other necessities required for his healthy development. The ultimate responsibility for his needs rested on my shoulders. Some parents may feel that because they were not involved in the procreation process they have no responsibility for the needs of the child. Once you commit to marriage, realize that you have a shared responsibility in raising the child — financial and emotional.

Now, what if you're blessed to receive child support? How should this money be handled? Include this money with the other family earnings. Remember, child support is not just for buying the kids clothes and toys. Child support also includes housing, meals, school, etc. It will be much easier if the child support is combined with the rest of the family finances. Separating this money for a specific child can create tension in the home and marriage. Any money coming into the house should be treated as family property. However, circumstances may require that a portion of the support remain separate. If that's the case, both spouses should clearly understand the amount and reason for the division.

Let's analyze a couple of examples. A spouse receives $600 per month in child support. This money should be included with the income earned by the parents and then used to manage the household expenses. If this money is separated for a specific child, it can create enmity between the stepparent and child and conflict with the other children in the home. Children are the first to notice preferential or different treatment. If one child appears to be more financially favored than the others, you can bet the competition will begin. All children should be treated equally, regardless of child support. Avoid this conflict upfront because you will have plenty of other issues to address. Also, it is unfair to expect your spouse to be responsible for your child's well being and keep money separated from him or her.

Let's look at another scenario. The mother has decided to be solely responsible for her children's needs. She does not expect her new husband to contribute to the financial costs of rearing her biological children. What potential problems can occur?

Another area of discussion is your credit history. Your joint credit status will determine the terms you receive for home loans, car loans, credit cards and employment opportunities. It is not uncommon for one spouse to have a history of paying bills on time and the other spouse to have a negative credit record. When applying for credit, you may receive unfavorable terms, but remember; derogatory credit is a temporary situation. Negative history comes off your report in seven years (ten years for bankruptcy). During this gestation period, establish a budget and spending plan. Pay all of the expenses on time and improve the negative credit rating. Find out if any credit arrangements from a divorce exist. Non-payment of accounts from your ex-spouse can affect you and your new spouse. Wisdom abounds in reviewing your credit reports so that no surprises spring up in the future. You are entitled to a free credit report from each credit bureau once a year. Just make sure you visit the correct website for this information — annualcreditreport.com. Imposter websites market free credit reports, but eventually charge a fee.

Estate planning can be tricky in a blended family. How will the assets transfer upon death? This decision may not be easy, unless you have decided that all the children will be treated equally. Some parents may want to keep certain assets in their family bloodline. The couple must work through these issues; otherwise the state will determine how your hard-earned assets transfer. Save your family the hassle and plan now.

You can unintentionally disinherit your children if you do not plan correctly. Let me give you an example. If the transference of your assets has not been finalized prior to you reaching the pearly gates, your ex-spouse will be the court-appointed manager of the assets you wanted to leave to the children. And if that's not enough to make your toes curl, your ex-spouse will also receive your inheritance, if he or she is unmarried and without children, and your children predecease you. Your ex is considered the next-of-kin for your children. No way! Way!

To protect your new spouse when a prenuptial agreement is not in place, consider re-titling your assets in both your names.

Also, rename the beneficiaries on your life insurance policies and retirement accounts. But be careful, if you predecease your spouse, you can disinherit your children. Your spouse will receive your assets and then their children or new spouse are next in line to receive the inheritance upon your death. I highly recommend consulting a qualified estate-planning attorney to discuss these issues.

The last topic to consider is Social Security benefits. A keynote to mention is that you are not eligible for your ex-spouse's benefits if you remarry before age sixty. You will be eligible under your new spouse's benefits though. If your own Social Security benefits are higher than your spouse's, you will receive the higher benefit amount. If you remarry after age sixty, you have the option of choosing the higher benefit of your current or former spouse. This selection applies if you are a disabled widow or a disabled surviving former spouse who marries after age fifty. If your new spouse is receiving Social Security benefits and you have been married for a least one year, or you are taking care of your spouse's child under the age of sixteen, you can receive benefits based on your spouse's wage record. For more information, contact the Social Security Administration.

As you can see, I am a firm believer in combining assets and expenses when a couple becomes one flesh. With a few exceptions, my experience has proven that this process works better when both spouses are in agreement. Handling debt, credit, college funding and other financial issues tends to gel easier. These matters are best discussed prior to marriage. If you are already married, communicate with each other as soon as possible. Money tends to be one of the primary reasons for separation. Get a hold of it now and it will not be a roadblock for your marriage in the future.

Mojitos Before 4

By Wendy Hart Beckman

When I worked for a diversity consultant, we used to warn our clients about focusing on obvious differences (such as gender, age and race) and overlooking other less-obvious areas for potential misunderstanding (such as personality types, religion and job classification). We used the "Four Layers of Diversity" described by Lee Gardenswartz and Anita Rowe to show the visible and invisible differences that cause friction. We called their diagram the diversity wheel — and I'm seeing diversity wheels spinning in my blended and reblended family. Let me tell you about my family. Sit back and relax — this gets complicated.

My sister was already with husband number two when I got married in the 80s. By the 90s, my brother had left wife number one and then married number two in the 2000s. My sister is now looking for husband number three.

On my husband's side, there's only one remarriage, but that union has redefined "blended." Steve's middle sister, Mary Kay, remarried a couple of years ago after a painful divorce from an absentee husband who wouldn't leave. Mary Kay's new husband wasn't so lucky as to lose his spouse through court decree. He woke up one morning, beside the body of his beloved wife. Within a year, his three sons — two in their 20s, one in his 30s — went from grieving their suddenly, deceased mother to welcoming a stepmother barely older than they.

The youngest son then further added to life's major stress events by moving from the home he shared with his fiancée, Christine (and her child), to marriage — to Letícia. Even her name was a shock: her nickname is Letí, pronounced "lechy" — as in lech or lecherous. It seemed like a bad sign.

I was taken aback at how quickly the youngest son had jumped from one relationship to another. The older brothers were unsettled that their little brother had bucked Latino tradition by marrying first — and so soon. Meanwhile, the men in my husband's family were startled at Letí's ankle tattoo and how gracefully her athletic legs walked out each time she left the room to smoke. But they are men, after all, so they soon welcomed Letí with open arms and hot blood. There's certainly nothing inappropriate going on, but she seems to bring people's emotions to a boil.

Letí is the kind of woman who women would love to hate, but with guilt. She's as charming as her teeth are white. Both charm and teeth flashed easily and frequently. Her dynamic figure introduced cropped tops, low-riders and tattoos into my in-laws' staid German household.

That same, sedate German household played salsa music at Thanksgiving. This might not seem so odd, except that I remember a couple of instances where my mother-in-law asked her hubby to turn off any background music during the meal. My father-in-law sighed and turned off his Debussy or Chopin or whatever classical piece was playing softly. However, in a well-intentioned attempt to welcome his new Cuban-American son-in-law, Bernie, my father-in-law played Latino tunes during dinner. And no word came from his wife.

Bernie and I once discussed what it was like to jump into the big Beckman machine. At least I came from a similar background (some German-American in me) if not the same region or Christian denomination as the Beckmans. On the other hand, Bernie shared Catholicism with his new in-laws, but he came from a Latino culture, and also had a whole family culture of his own. We laughed one day at how in the Beckman household, it is *verboten* to drink alcoholic beverages before 4 p.m. — cocktail hour. Bernie chuckled and said, "I'm Cuban — it's *always* cocktail hour!" We both agreed that our shared in-laws had gone to extremes in their attempts to make us part of their family.

"But I don't think they realize that they have now become a part of *my* family too," Bernie said. He brought me up cold. They now needed to enmesh themselves in someone else's tapestry.

In a mythical first marriage, people get married young, with no baggage of kids or culture, no houses to sell, no habits to break. But we know in real life that sometimes it doesn't even happen that way the first time around. The second (or third) time around surely entails more careful interweaving of the families. Newlyweds work out who gets them for Thanksgiving and Christmas or Passover and Hanukkah or whenever their traditions demand attendance at family functions. Oldlyweds have to work out who gets them, their kids, their grandchildren — and many other assorted details.

It came to me that our comic reference to the Beckmans as a machine was appropriate. My huge Beckman family is like a set of gears. Mary Kay was one cog on one big wheel, attached to her first husband, who was a cog on his own wheel. That wheel was removed and for awhile, Mary Kay's cog was unmatched. She only dealt with her place as a cog on her parents' wheel. Then along came Bernie. His cog matched up with hers, but wait — he had smaller cogs on *his* wheel! And now they're all in motion, trying to get in synch with the Beckman wheel.

An analogy often used in the diversity circuit is the comparison of a stew (like the old melting pot), a salad bar and

V-8 juice. Well, throwing your relatives into a blended family and hitting the "smoothie" button doesn't produce one homogeneous, happy mix that comes out tasting and looking the same. Nor should we really want it to.

Whether your drink is tomato juice, virgin daiquiri or mojitos before 4, blended families offer us a chance to experience new sensations and learn about new people. Sometimes those people are from a continent away; sometimes they're your new sons and daughters. As for me, I've learned that young women who smoke can be great people that just differ from my standards. Who knows — perhaps she thinks as negatively of my obesity as I think of her smoking? We don't let these personal differences get in the way of developing our cordial relationship. We are now family.

The Honeymoon Is Over His Perspective

By Craig Coleman, Sr.

On July 2, 1994, I made one of the most important and smartest decisions in my life. I married the love of my life. The topic of blended or stepfamilies was not discussed in our pre-marital counseling. Valerie and I did not know, nor were we prepared for what laid ahead for us.

I was twenty-nine years old and trying to acclimate to civilian life after eight years of active duty. I brought three children into my second marriage. My wife on the other hand, the mother of two boys, was college educated and worked in corporate America as an engineer. Two totally different backgrounds and yet, by the grace of God, we have managed to stay together all these years.

Before the wedding, we decided to raise and treat the kids equally. We would not tolerate differences between hers and mine: all of them were ours. Shortly after the honeymoon, I'm sure like most couples entering a blended family, reality kicked in. Living in different households with different sets of rules, we soon realized that blending was not going to be as easy as we hoped.

My ex had different beliefs and parenting skills. When my son and daughter visited, conflict erupted. They were used to doing things that we did not allow in our home; watching secular music videos, talking back and fighting with one another. When my wife corrected them, I often got a phone call from my ex. She informed me that Valerie was not permitted to correct her daughter. I had a choice to make: oblige her demands and give my kids preferential treatment or stand by the rules we established for our house. I stood by our rules at the expense of time with my children. I made it quite clear that I was not going to silence my wife in her own home. When I asked my ex if she would allow a child to dictate rules in her house, she quickly replied, "H*** no." Her comment validated my point and the conversation ended.

At that time, I worked a nontraditional job and my off days fell in the middle of the week. Since standard visitation was set for weekends, and my ex refused to compromise for weekday visits, Valerie would have to be the primary guardian. Given the strained relationship between my wife and daughter, I knew that was not going to work. Over time, my son continued to stay on a regular basis, but my daughter's visits dwindled. When she did come over, and Valerie joined us, my daughter complained to her mother that she did not get my undivided attention. I conversed with my ex over the phone and then shared this concern with Valerie. Upon the next visit, Val separated herself so that I could spend quality time with my daughter. The next complaint to my ex was that Valerie didn't want to have anything to do with my daughter when she came to visit. This volley back and forth continued for quite some time. A crazy, vicious cycle that frustrated Valerie and left me feeling like the last man standing in a game of artillery. All alone with opponents bombarding me from every side.

Rubber Band Man

As time passed, my relationship with my daughter was pathetic at best, so I dedicated more time with her. Because our cash flow was restricted, I didn't have extra money to hang out with the kids. As a result, my time with them was either at their home or mine. Valerie was uncomfortable with me sitting at my ex's house and my daughter did not want to come to my home. She did not want to have to interact with my wife. After several visits at the homes of family and friends, I reached my threshold. I felt like a rubber band stretched in all directions, just about to rip. Enough was enough.

Several times a year, my wife had out-of-town business trips. I used these opportunities to bring my son and daughter to my house. Valerie and I never discussed what I felt was my only option. On one occasion, my teenage daughter answered the phone when Valerie called home. The fireworks started.

"Hello?"

"Who is this?" Valerie asked.

"Dad, telephone."

"Hello?" I said.

"Craig, who answered the phone?"

"My daughter."

"I thought we agreed that she would not come to the house, if she refused to follow the rules. You're teaching her that it's okay to disrespect me."

"Well baby, how can she disrespect you, if you're not here?"

"That's a cop out. If she can't come over when I'm home, then she doesn't need to come over when I'm gone. It's like you're sneaking your mistress in the back door, when I walk out the front. That's not right."

"But it's the only time I can spend with my daughter at our house."

"That's not true. She's always had the option to come to the house. She just doesn't want to have to be bothered with me and you're encouraging it."

On at least two other occasions, I brought my daughter to the house despite my wife's request. Needless to say, it had a negative effect on our marriage.

You see, I felt like I was in a lose-lose situation. How do I maintain my status as a loving husband, best friend and protector to my queen and still be a decent father to my princess? I wanted to be more than a check-on-the-first-of-the-month father. I committed long ago that my relationship with my children would be more than just financial. I have several friends who pay support and think that's sufficient, but time spent has more importance than money. From my late pastor's example, the key to maintaining a good family relationship is through time together, prayer and the Word of God.

> *Trust in the Lord with all your heart, and lean not on your own understanding.*
> ~ Proverbs 3:5

"Lord, You are the King of kings and the Lord of lords. Please forgive me for anything that I have done that has displeased You. I now understand that this marriage covenant is not about my wife and me, but rather my relationship with You. Lord, protect my family and give us balance. Show me how to love and respect my queen. Teach me how to support her. And Father, show me how to build a better relationship with my princess and to keep her covered the way a father should."

Your biological children are part of a bloodline that cannot be severed, but the promise you made to your spouse can be easily broken. Focus on reinforcing the foundation of your marriage and holdfast to the covenant you made with your spouse and God.

One Bite at a Time
Her Perspective

By Valerie L. Coleman

With the car engine running and tears streaming down my cheeks, I decided to give my marriage one more try. I called my friend for prayer.

"Buffy, I can't take it anymore. It's been eleven years and his daughter still doesn't respect me." I fastened the seat belt to expedite my getaway.

"What's wrong Val?"

"It's like Craig just doesn't get it. She says and does things that are so disrespectful and mean. And when I mention it to him, he tells me that I'm the adult and the Christian." I rummaged through the armrest console for some tissue. "I'd never let my boys treat him like that."

"So tell me what happened." Her gentle voice quieted my tormented heart.

"Well, the other day all of the kids were over — a couple of nieces, Junior and our Godson, Boogie. As usual, the kids were up and down the steps, running through the house. Boogie and I were in the family room when the doorbell rang."

"Okay, so who was at the door?"

"Well, Boogie had just fallen asleep in my lap." My voice trembled. "I was going to lay him on the couch, when the stampede raced to the door."

"You okay?"

"Yeah. I'm okay." I blew my nose and continued. "Now, you know that I can see the front door from the family room, right?"

"Yeah, it's a clear shot. So?"

"So I'm still sitting on the couch trying to see who's at the door because all of the kids are parading around like the Energizer bunny." I revved the engine. "Before I could acknowledge her, she rolled her eyes, threw her hands on her hips, sucked her teeth and asked the kids, 'Is my daddy here?' Like I was not in the room."

"Oh, that was not good."

"Not good. If I didn't have Boogie in my lap, I may ha—"

"Let's not even go there. Be thankful that he was in your lap."

"You're right. I don't mean to sound petty, but this has been going on far too long. She'll call and then hang up if I answer the phone. And the things that she's said to me and about me are hurtful. I've never done anything to make her hate me."

"She doesn't hate you. She just wants to make sure that she doesn't lose her place as daddy's little girl."

"And I can appreciate that. I don't want to be his little girl, I'm his wife. But this is my queendom and I expect to be respected. I walk on eggshells to keep the peace. I feel like a prisoner in my own home. No one comes over here talking crazy to me, but her. And Craig does nothing about it."

"He probably feels like he's being pulled in every direction."

"Yeah, so do I. It's like having my arms and legs tied to four horses. Then the enemy slaps them and they charge off in different directions. I'm being ripped apart from the inside." I grabbed the last tissue.

"Well, how old is she? Maybe she's too young to know better."

"Sorry, but I am not going out like that. Whether two or twenty-two, a child needs to know his or her place in the family. She is eighteen and old enough to know better." I dabbed at the tears. "Look, I just called you for prayer. I'm at my wit's end. I'm in the driveway, ready to leave and never come back. If she wants her daddy, she can have him. I don't have anymore fight in me." I held the phone toward the dashboard and revved the engine again.

"Lord, we thank You for being our source and our sustainer. You are the God of more than enough. We know that You have ordained this marriage and we ask that You bring peace to this family. You have designated Valerie to set the atmosphere in her home and she has created an environment of warmth and love. Lord, let everyone that enters her home come in peace."

My dear, sweet friend prayed for another ten minutes. By the time she finished, tears cascaded down my cheeks and showered the steering wheel. "Thanks, Buffy."

"Be encouraged, Val. Things will get better."

I turned off the car and went inside the house. *Lord, I need Your help.* The revelation struck me like the slam of a judge's gavel. I've been running to my husband with my concerns about the marriage, the kids, the ex. He's just as torn and frustrated as I am. I need to go straight to the Father.

"Hey, babe. Where have you been?" Craig greeted me at the door.

"Getting some fresh air." I kissed my king and then headed for my secret place. I needed some one-on-one time with my Daddy. Everyday for two weeks, I came home from work and went to my prayer closet. Prostrate before the Lord, I asked Him to help me be a better stepmother and wife. On the third day of my spiritual petitioning, I overheard Craig on the telephone.

"Look, baby girl, I love you with all my heart. You know that, right? Okay, then tell me this, who is your favorite teacher? Just answer the question." He paused. "And what makes Mrs. Johnson special?" By this time, my ears perked up like a hunting dog that spotted the fox.

"So, you like Mrs. Johnson because she sincerely cares about you. That's fair. Now, I assume that with that 'like' comes respect, right?" I pretended to be engaged in *Law & Order*, as he continued. "I trust your judgment of character. So, since you like and respect Mrs. Johnson, then I do too. Not because I know her, but because you know her. Sound reasonable? Good. Now, I need you to do me a small favor. Show my wife the same respect you show Mrs. Johnson. Not because you know her, but because I know her. She sincerely cares about you. Trust my judgment."

With my bottom jaw on the floor and eyes wide open, I shifted in the chair. A smile washed across my face. *Okay, Lord, I get it. Take it to You.*

Since that conversation, our relationship has improved. Not in leaps and bounds, but small steps in the right direction. We have brief conversations on the phone and she's even asked for my opinion a couple of times. We're eating the elephant one bite at a time.

My Dog

By Lucinda Greene

The Amber alert blared over the radio station. "Two African-American girls, both about five-feet tall and weighing eighty to ninety pounds. Last seen at the local Boys Club leaving with their father. If you have any information on these girls, please call the Hamilton, Ohio police department."

The long Cadillac sped up and I looked around to my sister sitting in the front seat. I rummaged through the garbage bag on the back seat next to me. "Daddy, why are our clothes in this bag?"

"I'm washing them for you," he wiped the sweat from his brow.

"But you said that we were going to eat." I bit my nails. "And Momma has a washer and dryer at home."

My sister cried, "I want my Momma." Daddy patted her leg and shushed her. He didn't really care about us. We hadn't seen him in weeks and when he finally called, I told him everything. Momma told me not to put her business on the street, but when her business pertained to me, I said and did what I wanted.

"Momma's got a new boyfriend," I had said to Daddy as a slight grin creased my lips.

"Oh really. What's his name?"

"Mac," I paused. "But I don't like him." Mac was always nice to my sister and me. He bought us whatever we wanted without hesitation. My dislike for him had nothing to do with his character; I just didn't want to see Momma with no one but Daddy. As planned, Daddy reacted. We bolted down the highway with the cry baby at maximum volume.

"Come on, baby girl," Daddy reached for my sister. "Your mother told me to pick you up from the club today."

"I don't want to go," she said, with tears in motion. "Momma said that we are only allowed to leave with Godmommy and her."

"Why are you acting like a baby?" I elbowed my sister in the side. "Ain't you glad to see Daddy? He said he was going to take us to McDonald's. Let's go."

"But I don't want to go."

"Wimp. You're just a big wimp." I crossed my arms and stomped my feet.

She tried to stifle her tears. "I'm not a wimp," she sniffled and walked toward the car. "Come on. I got front."

I didn't care that the police were looking for us. I missed my daddy and liked being with him. So we continued to ride in the hot Caddy. "Daddy, when are we going to eat?"

He looked at me through the rear-view mirror. "As soon as we get there!" I rolled my eyes at him and slapped the seat. We pulled over to a small restaurant. We ordered hamburgers and fries and ate in silence. As soon as we finished, Daddy let us call Momma from a payphone.

"Momma, come get us," my sister said. "I want to come home." She paused, "Yes ma'am. It's kind of white and has a lot of win—"

Daddy snatched the phone. "If you want to talk to the girls, you're going to have to stop asking them questions about where we are. I am not going to hurt my own kids." He turned his back to us so we couldn't hear him cuss at Momma. It didn't work.

"Here," he held the phone out to me. "Your mother wants to talk to you." Before he let me take the phone, he covered it and said, "Don't try to tell her where we are."

"Okay." I took the phone. "Hi, Momma."

"I love you baby."

"I love you too, Momma."

"I'll be there to get you so—"

"Momma, are you going to feed my dog for me?"

"I know at least you're going to be all right. Take care of your sister you hear?"

"I will, but she keeps crying and getting on my nerves." I cut my eyes at my sister.

"Do you know where you are?"

"Yeah, it's the Denny's on Highway 202." My father snatched the phone and hung it up. I rolled my eyes at him again. We piled in the car and as soon as he drove out the parking lot, my sister cried. I fell asleep. When I opened my eyes, the car pulled up to my aunt's house in Little Rock, Arkansas.

After a brief greeting to my aunt and uncle, Daddy put us to bed. My sister cried the entire time. "What is wrong with you?" I asked, as I tried to get comfortable in the twin bed.

"I want Momma."

"She'll be here in a little while. Now will you please, please stop crying?" I might as well have asked a forest fire to stop raging. She hollered louder, so I got up to spend some time with my family. My aunt and uncle sat at the kitchen table, but Daddy wasn't in the room. "Where's my daddy?"

"He'll be back in a few days," my aunt said. I tilted my head, crinkled my forehead and looked at them. "Now, give Aunty a hug and a kiss."

I kissed her and then hugged my uncle. "Where are my cousins?"

"They're over their grandmother's house."

"Oh, well do you think it will be okay if I call my momma?"

My uncle decided to join the conversation. "Can you wait until the morning?"

"I want to see if she fed my dog." My aunt looked at my uncle. He shrugged as if to say okay, so I took the phone into the room with me.

"Call Momma, cry baby." She whined to Momma for a few minutes, then I took the phone to my aunt.

"He left them here with us," she told my mother.

I stomped back to the bedroom and slammed the door. Why did Daddy kidnap us just to leave us here with our aunt and uncle? Wasn't seeing them at the family reunion enough? My sister sniffled and snorted, so I got into bed with her. She fell asleep.

Early the next morning, my sister woke me up asking a thousand questions about Daddy. "Why did he bring us here?"

"Huh?" I rolled over.

"What was he thinking when he brought us all the way out here?"

"Shh. I'm trying to sleep," I threw the pillow over my head.

"Why did he lie and say Momma told him to take us?" She nudged me.

"Girl, please."

"Well I want to know why."

"Then you need to start speaking up for yourself." The aroma of sizzling pork bacon crept under the bedroom door. My stomach growled. I looked at my sister and she licked her lips. We jumped out of bed, got dressed and ran to the kitchen. Surprise!

Momma and Mac sat at the table. My sister ran to Momma and wrapped her arms around her. They both cried like newborn babies slapped by the doctor. Mac had his arms outstretched for me. I waved at him and sat at the table. Momma came over and picked me up. She squeezed me until my belly rumbled. She whispered in my ear, "Be nice."

I gave her a big kiss and asked, "Momma, did you bring my dog?"

"You'll see him soon enough. You're going home today."

"I have to wait for Daddy to get back." Momma put me down.

"Time to eat," she said. My aunt and uncle looked like they just saw a ten-foot mouse run across the kitchen floor. I guess, like me, they knew Daddy was not coming back. My sister jumped in the seat next to Momma. So, with only six chairs at the table, I was stuck next to Mac.

"Did you sleep okay last night?" he said. "I know how you like to —"

"Aunty, what time is Daddy coming back?"

"Well, uh sweetie, I don't know exactly." From the corner of my eye, I saw Mac tighten his lips. He mumbled something under his breath.

After breakfast, we walked into the living room. Momma said, "All right girls, get your things. We're heading home."

"I'm not going back with you guys. I'm going to wait on my daddy to come and get me." As I finished my comment, my sister ran and got our stuff.

"You ain't running nothing but your mouth. We have a ten-hour drive ahead of us and I don't need anymore pressure on me."

"Aunty, is it okay if I stay here until my dad—?"

"I am the mother and you will do what I tell you to do." Without flinching, I continued to look at my aunt for an answer. Silence. No one said a word, while I had a stand-off with my mother. Then Daddy walked in the house.

"Momma, please don't let Daddy take us again," the big baby whined.

"Baby girl, are you afraid of me?" Daddy knelt down and touched her arm.

"No, I just want to live with Momma."

Daddy turned to me. "Sissy, what do you want to do?"

"I want to stay with you Daddy." I ran and jumped in his arms.

"The courts said that I have custody." Momma stood and put her hands on her hips. "Besides, how are you going to take care of a child from jail?"

"Who's going to jail?" Daddy stood.

"You," she said and pointed at my daddy.

Mac stood and held Momma's hand. "Honey, calm down." The whiner fell into a full rage and hollered louder than ever. Daddy yelled some nasty words at Momma and of course, she yelled some back at him.

My aunt stood to defend Momma. "Robert! You shouldn't say those types of things to her, especially in front of the girls!"

My uncle grabbed his wife's hand and pulled her down to the chair. "Sit down and stay out of this."

Momma and Daddy continued to argue while Mac tried to calm things down. I left the room and walked into the kitchen to find a snack. My aunt made one last attempt to stop the madness. "Just let Sissy stay with us for a few days. I'll send her home by bus." I ran back into the living room.

Momma looked at Daddy, then at Mac. Mac shrugged and nodded. "Okay," Momma said as she turned to Daddy. "But you have got to turn yourself into the police."

"Okay. Okay. I will. But let me spend today with my girl. I'll turn myself in tomorrow." With all the confusion settled, the three of them got into Mac's car.

I peeked into the backseat. My sister grinned like she just got a super-sized lollipop. "You make sure you feed my dog."

"I will."

"No, you've got to promise."

"I promise," she said, as she buckled her seat belt. "Bye, Sissy. Let's go Momma."

My cousins finally came home from their grandmother's house. We laughed, played and had a great time, until Momma called. "Are you ready to come home?"

"No. I'm still playing with my cousins."

"Take your time, but you have to be home before school starts."

"Okay, Momma. Thanks. Can I talk to my sister?"

"Sure baby." The phone went silent for a minute.

"Hello?"

"You been feeding my dog?"

"Yes. When are you coming home?"

"I'll be home soon. Why?"

"Because I'm tired of playing with your dog. I'm ready to play with you." She cried. "I miss you."

"Put Momma back on the phone." I tapped my fingers on the phone. "Momma, I want to stay just a little while longer. Please."

"All right, Sissy. I'll pick you up this weekend."

Momma came as promised, but I was not ready to go yet. We sat on the living room couch as I convinced her to let me go to school in Arkansas with my cousins.

"You know, you're making some difficult choices for a child of your age. I need you to understand that with choices, comes responsibility. Life is nothing but a series of choices. You can choose to do right or you can choose to do wrong. I pray that you always choose to do right." Momma stroked my hair, stared at me, then continued. "I'll let you stay here, until you're ready to come home on your own. I'm not going to make that decision for you."

"Thanks, Momma." My face lit up the room like the golden arches light the way to McDonald's.

"And when you do choose to come home, know that I have rules — rules that you will follow."

"Yes ma'am."

"First and foremost, you will respect my house and you will respect Mac."

What'd she say that for? "I can't respect a man that I don't like."

"Well, young lady, you don't have to like him, but you will respect him." She sat up straight, adjusted her skirt and then cleared her throat. "I'm with child."

"No!" I jumped off the couch. "How could you have another child? You're trying to replace me!" Tears ran down my cheeks.

"Baby, I'm not trying to replace you. I could never do that." She took my hand and sat me on her lap. "I will always love you. No one could ever replace you." She nestled my head to her bosom. "You know that you're my special child. You're so smart and full of wisdom — my independent baby. Everybody thinks you're the oldest. You have a lot of your daddy's hustle in you and I like that. You can come home anytime you want."

Momma left that weekend and I stayed with my aunt, uncle and cousins. Daddy turned himself in, but he didn't do any time. His lawyer got him off because it was his visitation weekend. And since crossing state lines was not discussed in the custody battle, he was within his rights to take us where he wanted. I talked to my daddy on the phone every other day and he sent money to my aunt and uncle on a regular basis.

Momma had the baby and she married Mac. My sister wrote me everyday. I wrote her back once a month or so. Two years into my family reunion vacation, I called my daddy. "Daddy, you've got to take me home. I'm ready to go now."

"Sissy, you're going to have to wait until the weekend. I've got to —"

"What do you mean I have to wait until the weekend? I'm ready to go now." I slammed the phone down, walked away and then returned. "Are you still there?"

"Young lady, you do not have the right to —"

"I said that I am ready to go. I know that you don't care about me, but I still love you. I didn't get mad at you for stealing us from Momma. I'm not even mad that you're not here with me everyday. I know the only reason you came and snatched us was because you were jealous that Momma had another man."

Daddy drove in from Texas that night and I got to Momma's house the next afternoon. See I had to go home, my dog died.

Two Children, No Mother; Tag, You're It

By Antwonette Caddell

For weeks on end, I called the hospital morgue. Needing to know if she was dead was like descabbing an infected wound; painful, but necessary.

"No ma'am. We don't have any Jane Does that fit that description."

As children, my big sister took care of me. When the night sounds frightened me, she let me sleep with her. When I broke Mother's favorite dish, she took the blame and the inevitable whipping. She protected me from the playground bullies. Now, she needed me to protect her, but her bullies weren't after her lunch or milk money, and I didn't know how to fight them off.

With renewed hope, I trudged downtown. My sister disappeared for days and weeks at a time, but she had never been gone for four months. Armed with a picture of my sibling, I walked the streets for hours. Stepping over cardboard condos, I showed the picture to fiends and addicts. As the sun settled on the city's skyline, I stopped by the police station, filed a missing persons report and left the picture. When I got home, I prayed.

For the next three months, I made weekly calls to the police station. Nothing. One night around midnight, the phone rang. *Oh Lord, it's late, the phone's ringing. She's dead.* The phone rang three times before I lifted the receiver to my ear. Without saying a word, I listened for the bad report.

"Myia?" A weak voice called out to me. I remained silent. "Myia, it's me, Sissy."

"Thank You God," I whispered with tears running down my face. "Where are you, Sissy?"

"I'm at the bus station. Can you pick me up?"

"I'm on my way." I dropped the phone, grabbed my keys and ran out the door in my pajamas. I sped through red lights and stop signs. At the station, I slammed my car in park and caused the engine to stall. I ran up and down the aisles. "Sissy! Sissy, where are you?"

She stepped out of the restroom. Her matted hair and tattered clothes didn't compare to the wear that crawled on her face. She had aged ten years. She walked toward me and tried to wrap her arms around me. I stepped back.

"What's wrong?"

"Nothing, I'm all right." I stared at the stranger in front of me. Decayed teeth dangled in her mouth. Her breath smelled like a week-old rotting carcass. She looked like a malnourished Ethiopian child — frail, shriveled body and an inflated stomach.

"Where'd you park?" She clawed at her forearms. "Will you carry these for me?"

Stunned, I grabbed her bags. My mind raced, as we walked to the car. *Where have you been?* I didn't want to make her feel bad or uncomfortable, so I kept my mouth shut and drew my own conclusions.

"You hungry?" I asked, as we walked into the front door.

"No, I'm tired. I'll just go up to bed, if that's okay with you."

"Sure, I'll see you in the morning." I kissed her cheek and watched her waddle up the stairs.

I riffled around in the kitchen for a few minutes to give her time to settle into bed. Then I went to my bedroom and prayed.

"Lord, Thank You for bringing my sister home. I knew that You would keep her safe. And Lord, protect the child that she's carrying. Help it to be okay. Now, Father, I ask that You bridle my tongue and guard my heart. Give me the words to say to encourage Sissy. I don't want to nag and frustrate her. God keep me from belittling, embarrassing or offending her."

To catch up with dear ol' sis, I took a personal day from work. When she got up at noon, I cooked her favorite breakfast: pecan pancakes, eggs — scrambled hard — and turkey bacon. I sat at the table beside her to put us on the same level. We needed to have a woman-to-woman talk and I needed to minimize all barriers to effective communication. But before I could get a word out, she had woofed down her food.

"Can you fix me some more?"

"So what are you going to do about your situation?" I prepared a second helping and placed it in front of her.

"What situation? My baby ain't no situation." She pushed the plate away. "And I'm keeping it."

"Hold on, Sissy. I wasn't saying get rid of the baby. I just wanted to know how you plan to raise it. Is the father going to be any help?" I slid the plate back to her.

"I'm not sure who the father is."

A chill ran through me that could have frozen the Sahara Desert. "You are an irresponsible, low life and if you don't do something with your life I am going to kick you out on that proud little butt of yours."

Her glazed eyes watered. "I knew I shouldn't have called you. You act just like Mama. She's why I'm in the streets now. Just because I didn't go to college and don't work for some big company doesn't make me less than you." She stood and pointed at me. "Look at you. Your life is not so spectacular either. You come home to an empty house. You're so involved in your work that you don't even have time for a man."

"Well maybe if you got yourself involved in something other than sex and drugs you wouldn't be in the predicament that you're in."

"That's right; I forgot that you're perfect. Well, Miss Perfection, let's not forget the predicaments you've been in. I came to your rescue every time, but now you want to be my judge and jury just because I did something that you don't approve of." Tears streamed down her face.

"I'm not judging you. I just want you to start making good decisions."

"The only bad decision I made was coming back here. I'll be gone by morning and I don't want anything else from you." She stormed up the stairs and slammed the bedroom door.

"Ooo, I am so stupid," I said, as I slapped my forehead. I replayed the conversation in my head and realized that I did sound like my mother. Shame jumped on my shoulders like a lion pouncing on its prey. I let my anger control the conversation and I silenced God.

"Let me go for a walk and cool down. Then I'll talk to her again." I wrapped her plate in foil and put it in the refrigerator. "I'm sorry Lord." By the time I got home, Sissy was gone and so was my Visa. I guess she needed something from me after all.

A month later I received a phone call from the credit card company. "Miss Caddell, there has been some unusual activity on your card. We're just calling to verify that you authorized these purchases."

"What was purchased?"

"A bus ticket to Chicago, a baby bed, baby clothes and food."

"I used the card to help out my sister. Thanks for calling." I approved the purchases and paid off the card. I didn't cancel the only link I had to my sister. As long as she charged things on it, I knew where she was and that she and the baby were okay.

~ ~ ~ ~ ~ ~ ~

Six months later, I received a letter from Sissy. She apologized for the things she had said and promised to pay me back. I searched the envelope for a return address and noticed something sticking out of it — a picture of my niece. With her chubby cheeks and curly hair, she looked just like Sissy at that age. On the back of the picture, she wrote, "To my favorite auntie with love Little Myia."

"She named her after me." I touched my heart and expelled a breath. I put the picture in my Bible under Psalm 91. My mother used to read us this protection verse every night.

An entire year passed before I heard from her again. "Myia, can I come home?"

"Yes! Go buy yourself a ticket and I'll meet you at the bus station."

"We're already at the station waiting on you."

I jumped up, grabbed my keys and ran out of the house half-dressed, just like the last time. And like last time, she was pregnant. *Lord, I will not fuss, and I will not say anything to hurt her or make her leave again.*

She waited outside with a bag in one hand and a baby in the other. I got out of the car and helped them.

"I'm sorry to call you out of the blue."

"It's no problem. I'm happy to do it." I looked around for her other things. "Where are the rest of the baby's things?" Judging by my credit card bills, she was missing at least three bags and a baby bed. We walked to the car in silence. "Do you want me to stop and get you two something to eat?"

"Would you mind dropping us off at home and bringing us something to eat?"

No, you must think I'm stupid. "Sure." I got them settled and then drove to not one, or two, but three different restaurants. Cravings. When I got home, her things were thrown all over the living room. I handed her the food and picked up the mess.

"Do you mind giving the baby a bath?"

"Not at all, it would be my honor and pleasure." I missed out on my niece's birth, first steps and first birthday, so I jumped at the opportunity to give her a bath. I whisked her in my arms and carried her upstairs to the bathroom, smooching on her all the way. With the water running, I took off her clothes.

"Pee-ew, you stink." I crinkled my nose and fanned the air. Little Myia giggled. I took off her pants and the stench gagged me. Filled with poop and pee, her diaper was weighted down and hung to her pudgy knees. With my lips curled tight, I hollered down the stairs to Sissy.

"Do you have anymore diapers for the baby?"

"No, I ran out of money a few days ago."

"Why didn't you charge some diapers like you charge everything else?"

"I didn't want to go over your limit."

Well, isn't that thoughtful. "Come give the baby a bath while I go to the store." I waited for her to waddle into the bathroom. "Do you need anything else?"

She pulled a list out of her bra. "Just a few things." I took the list, smiled at her and skipped to the store.

The next couple of weeks, I ran like an Olympic gold medalist trying to break a world record. I located a daycare and I took the baby there everyday. After a full day at work, I picked her up from the daycare and then came home to cook and clean. I gave my angel a bath, read her a story and then put her to bed. I turned my office into a pink nursery decorated with flowers and furnished it with a bed, dresser and changing table. I bought her educational toys and books. Daddy number two was not going to be in the picture either.

Sissy's daily routine consisted of eating and calling me at work to complain about not having anything to eat. She had gained about thirty pounds, so her feet hurt too much to cook. The smell from the cleaning products made her nauseous, so she couldn't clean up. Little Myia made too much noise, so she couldn't pick her up from the nursery when I worked late. I had to pay extra for the after-hours care.

I never complained. I didn't want her to leave and take my niece from me. That little girl had me wrapped around her finger. If she eyed something in the store, I bought it. Her laughter warmed my home. She never cried when we were together and she followed me wherever I went. If I grabbed my coat, she grabbed hers.

"Little Myia looks just like you."

"I think she looks more like you."

A month later, and two days before my birthday, my nephew was born. I stood at her bedside in the recovery room. "You want to name him?"

"You serious? You'll let me name him?"

"Yeah."

"Okay, I'll name him John, after Daddy."

"I like that. I was Daddy's little girl," she said with a smirk on her face.

"What are you going to do now?"

"I'm going to kick this habit and find me a job. My babies are depending on me."

"You can stay with me as long as you want." She looked up at me with dollar signs flashing in her eyes. "No charge."

"Thanks."

Two months later, she found a job. She struggled to be a good mother and provide for her kids, but she didn't make enough to pay the daycare expenses.

"Just drop me some money when you get paid and I'll take care of the rest." She gave me fifty dollars here and twenty dollars there. Not much, but at least she tried.

She came to church with me and had the kids baptized. We read the Bible to the kids at night and she read it for herself too. She ran into my room when she had a question and we talked for hours about the Word.

"I'm proud of you, Sissy. You have really turned your life around."

"Thanks. It's all because of you."

"No, it's all because of Jesus." I kissed her cheek. "I wish Mama could have seen this."

For three months, she stayed clear of drugs. For three months, I trusted her with my car. For three months, she kept a job and for three months, she brought home money and spent money on the kids. For three months, she went to church, prayed and studied the Bible. But on day 91, everything stopped and the lies started.

Because she had to be at work later than I did, she dropped me off at work and then drove to her job. We'd done it a dozen times without incident. This particular day, I had to catch a ride home with one of my co-workers. The daycare was two blocks from the house, so I walked to the daycare. The kids and I walked home and enjoyed the bright sun and gentle breeze.

"Let's cook dinner for your mommy." Little Myia pulled her chair to the sink and climbed up. She splashed in the water, as I rinsed vegetables for the salad. I fed the kids spaghetti and let them watch Nickelodeon. I picked up the phone.

"Hello, my name is Myia. I'm calling to see if Sissy, I mean Cassandra, has left work yet."

"She didn't come in today."

"Did she say why?"

"No, she didn't call in. When you see her, please have her pick up her last check."

Fear ripped through me. I ran to the kitchen and snatched my purse off the counter. My credit cards and checkbook were still there. I sprinted through the house. TV — check. Microwave — check. DVD player — check.

"Whew!" Relieved, I plopped on the couch and then jumped to my feet. "My car!"

I paced the floor and debated calling the police. "I'll give her some more time. She's probably running errands and lost track of time."

At eight o'clock, I put the kids in bed. For a few hours, I cleaned, paid bills, anything to keep the bad thoughts from bombarding my mind. By midnight, I nodded in front of the TV. The sharp jerk of my heavy neck woke me. I stomped to bed without praying for Sissy.

The next morning, I called my job, then the police. Like the times before, they were no help. "I'm sorry ma'am, but adults are not considered missing until they've been gone for more than forty-eight hours." I sighed. "There's nothing we can do."

"Okay then, I want to report my car as stolen."

"Since you gave her permission to use the car, it's not stolen. If she isn't back by tomorrow morning, please call us back."

She retuned home that evening right after dinner. I went about my motherly tasks without acknowledging her. I dressed the kids for bed, then went into my room and closed the door.

She knocked on my door. "Can I come in? I want to talk to you."

"I don't have anything to say to you. Just put my car keys by the door and leave."

She stood by the door for a while, then dropped the keys and went into her room. I ignored her for two days and refused to feed her for one. The Holy Spirit convicted me. "I'm sorry I've been ignoring you, Sissy."

"Oh, Myia. I'm the one that's sorry. I promise I won't do that again." We hugged.

"I am very disappointed in you." I stepped back and looked her in the eyes. "I don't know that I'll be able to trust you again." My hands went for my hips and then I slapped them to my sides. "Why did you mess up three months of being a good mother and having a job?"

"I'm still a good mother and I'll find another job."

"Where were you? Why didn't you call me?" I knew where she had been, but I wanted to hear her say it. I wanted her to hear how terrible it sounded bouncing off the walls. I wanted her to hear her voice tell me that getting high was more important than her children.

She stood in front of me with tears flowing. "You know where I was."

"No, tell me where you were." She did not reply. "You need to get your life straight before you mess up your kids' lives too."

Over the next two months, things got worse. Gone at least three days a week, she looked like the Grim Reaper when she did come home. Her facial features grayed and withered. She lost a couple more teeth. "Sissy, how can I help you?"

"Help? I don't need any help. What makes you think I need help?"

"Have you looked in the mirror lately?"

"There you go, sounding just like Mama. You know what, you're gonna die a lonely, bitter, maid just like Mama too."

"It's time for you to go." I planted my feet and pointed to the door. "I am not paying your way anymore. I am canceling the credit card so don't ask me or anyone else in the family for money. I am finished with you."

"If I have to leave, I'm taking the kids with me." She rocked her head and shifted her weight.

"I will call children's services and let them take the kids into custody before I give them to you." She stormed out the house.

~ ~ ~ ~ ~ ~ ~

Six weeks without a word from Sissy, then she showed up at my job. Filthy. She had on the same clothes she wore when she left. The lice parade in her tangled mane made my skin crawl. Embarrassed, I tried to hide behind a newspaper, as I walked by her.

"Myia, can you loan me some money?"

"Don't have any."

She dropped her head. "I'm sick and need a fix real bad."

"I'll take you to the hospital. They can help you."

"Just give me five dollars. I can get my own help."

"Yeah, I'm sure you can." I turned and walked away. I tapped on the elevator call button.

"Excuse me sir," Sissy engaged a suited gentleman in conversation. "I'll take good care of you for five dollars."

I darted from the elevator, yanked her arm, and pulled her outside the building. "What do you think you're doing?"

"Since you won't give me the money, I've got to look elsewhere."

I grabbed her by the arm and forced her in the car. "Don't you realize that you could get AIDS from having sex with men you don't know?"

"Are you going to give me the money or not?"

"Not." She jumped out of the car. I slammed on the brakes, ready for a foot pursuit, but she hurdled a fence and disappeared.

~ ~ ~ ~ ~ ~ ~

A year passed before I saw her again. I watched the TV from the kitchen, as I cooked dinner.

"The Jane Doe is an African-American woman approximately forty years old." I dropped the knife and ran into the living room to turn up the volume. "She has black hair and a tattoo on her left leg." The reporter cupped her hand over the earpiece. "The tattoo reads 'Daddy's Little Angel.'" I called the babysitter to stay with the kids and I went down to the city morgue.

"Before you view the body, we need to ask you some questions."

"Go ahead." I rubbed my hands together.

"How old was your sister?"

"Twenty-five."

"And how long has she been missing?"

"Over a year." Tears creased the corners of my eyes. "Why do you need to know this?"

"Just one more question, ma'am. How long had she been on drugs?"

"One day too long."

The officer handed me a bag with her personal items. The jeans she had on the last time I saw her were tattered and torn. The shirt, mere rags. I pulled a picture of the kids playing out of the pocket.

"I don't need to see the body. I know the woman you found is my sister."

"We need you to fill out some papers." He directed me to a small office.

"I'll have the funeral home pick up her body in the morning" I walked out before the tears assaulted me.

As soon as I got in the car I broke down. For ten minutes I cried. I cried because I didn't have a sister anymore. I cried because her children didn't have a mother anymore. I cried because God failed me. I beat on the steering wheel.

Then, without warning, the tears dried. I realized that I didn't have to worry about where she was and if she was safe. She couldn't mess up her children's lives and kill their spirits by running back and forth between them and drugs. She's at peace. No more harm can come to her. She's in God's hands. I smiled.

A few days later, I laid my big sister to rest. The family came to pay their respects and meet her children. We sat at the kitchen table and ate food the saints had dropped by.

"Now that she's gone, you can finally rest, Myia," an aunt said, as she shoveled mac & cheese in her mouth.

A distant cousin added his unsolicited advice. "Yeah, you can live your own life now."

Like my sister ever held me back from doing what I wanted to do. I prayed more in the two days these kinfolk were at my house, than I did in a month when I didn't know where my sister was. When the fresh flowers wilted and the last relative pulled out of the driveway, reality slapped me in the face. Open-handed slap.

"I'm a mother." I stared out the front window. "I'm not just an aunt looking after them until their mother finds her way home; I am their mother." The demands of parenting rushed through my mind. Cook, clean and clothe them until they're eighteen. And if they go to college, it could be six more years. What if they want to go to law school or medical school?

Sweat beaded on my forehead. I paced the floor and wrung my hands together. I grabbed the phone, dialed 411 and then hung up.

"I don't even know their fathers' names." I knocked the phone off the table. "Sissy, what have you done to me? I was happy living by myself. I could come and go as I pleased. I could walk around my house naked and eat fast food every night." I collapsed on the couch and sobbed. "But now I have to cook a real meal every night and I have to be fully dressed when I walk around the house."

My head throbbed from worry and then peace settled in my spirit. "Wait a minute. I've been taking care of the kids for a couple of years now. This mothering thing isn't new to me. I can't let my babies go to a foster home, so if I don't take care of them, who will?"

Congratulations, you are the mother of a girl and a boy!!!

~ ~ ~ ~ ~ ~ ~

My sister died two years ago and I have been through a lot. Diapers, bandages on boo-boos, school clothes, new teeth, loose teeth, first steps, bike rides without training wheels, potty training and many, many sleepless nights. I wouldn't trade it for the world.

I remember asking the Lord to save my sister and bring her home. I asked Him to bless me with a family because my house was too big for one person. That was over five years ago. He might not come when you want Him, but He's right on time.

The Years Sown in Tears

By Karen M. Johnson

They that sow in tears shall reap in joy.
~ Psalm 126:5

Marta crawled out of bed, tired in body, but not in spirit. She had stayed up late the night before to add the final touches on her daughter's life book. A ritual she created years ago, Marta captured her children's memories in meticulous detail. She chose unique photo albums with great care and revealed a new book on their birthdays.

These photo albums represented all the years of hard work she put into life after divorce. These books recorded their pain and healing. Serious about keeping the albums in chronological order, she stored them in an enclosed bookcase. *No one better mess up my photo albums. I've worked too hard on these.*

The project she started to help her children cope often brought Marta to a place of peace. She reflected on the years in the form of faces and places. She needed to see the growth in her children: their progression from baby smiles to preteen poses.

"The kids are going to suffer. They're going to end up hating you," her ex-husband said, as he slammed the car door. "And you'll never find anyone who wants you." He sped away and yanked Marta's self-esteem in the process.

"Ladybug, get up! It's your birthday, Miss Fifteen," Marta said in a soft, sing-song voice. She nudged her daughter and then plopped down on the bed. "My grandmother always said, 'You can't get time back, so —'"

"So you better capture it," Ladybug said with her arms stretched to the ceiling.

Marta chuckled. "That's right, baby. Now get up before you miss the bus."

Through half-opened eyes, Ladybug found her way to the bathroom across the hall. As she splashed water on her face, she called out to her mother.

"Mommy, did Daddy call last night? He told me that he and Tracy were gonna take me shopping. You know I want those new Forces, right?" Ladybug flashed a big cheesy grin.

"You're special." Marta smiled and then rolled her eyes. "As sleepy as you are, you can still focus on shopping. No, baby he didn't call last night." Marta speculated that he was preoccupied with his newest companion, wife number three.

Ladybug and her older brother, Junior, had to make many adjustments. At three and six years old, they adapted to their father living in a different home.

"Now you have two houses," Marta said with great enthusiasm. She clapped her hands to coax happiness from her children. Just as they settled into their new home, they watched Marta pack clothes for a visit with their father.

"Daddy's here! Daddy's here," they said in unison, when their father pulled into the driveway. They jumped about the front room like kangaroos on pogo sticks. But when they saw "that lady" in the car, the enthusiasm fled and their faces dropped.

"Why can't we have time with Dad without her?" Junior threw his overnight bag on the floor. "He loves her more than he loves us."

"No baby, that's not true. Your father loves you very much." Marta understood that the children held out hope that their parents would get back together. But "that lady" symbolized the end of their optimism.

Anxious herself, Marta masked her feelings. She did not want the children to be affected by her apprehension. Will the kids be safe? Will he feed them? What if Senior and his new wife take the kids out of town on a so-called vacation and never come back? How will his wife treat the kids? Will she piggyback off his behavior or be jealous of his relationship with the children? Unfortunately, the latter was true.

Although unintentional, some stepmoms jockey for position against their stepchildren. Marta realized that the stepmom was trying to feel her way through too. She realized that the skills of discernment and understanding are necessary when dealing with the new stepmom. So instead of finding blame with "that lady," she asked the Lord for wisdom.

"I don't like her Mommy," Junior said. At nine years old, he had no difficulty expressing himself. "She doesn't do anything like a mommy should."

"What do you mean, baby?"

He counted on his fingers. "She doesn't read to us. She doesn't act like she wants to talk to us and her kids get all the stuff we should be getting."

"It'll get better. I promise." Marta kissed her son on the forehead and then went to her bedroom. "Lord, how in the world do I address this?" She released a deep sigh. "I don't want to condemn this new woman, but if my child is having such a hard time with this, how do I not say or do anything?" She knelt and talked with her Abba for guidance. "Help me to resolve any emotional damage I feel from the loss of my marriage. I need You to intervene in this earthly matter. Restore my mind so that I can focus on what You have for me. Give me the words to say to encourage and edify my children."

Ten years after their divorce, Marta asked Senior for a family meeting. She wanted to establish a forum for the families to come together and discuss issues. At the first meeting, tension hung in the air like the fog on Loch Ness. Awkward, difficult but effective. Although the new stepmom declined the invitation, Marta was hopeful that she would attend a subsequent meeting. Eventually, she did.

"Ladybug, your dad's on the phone," Marta said from down the hall. "Hurry up so you don't miss the bus. I can't drive anyone to school today!"

Ladybug popped out of her room and ran to the living room. She picked up the phone. "Happy birthday, Boogie-Woogie!" Senior put on the cartoon voice he reserved just for her.

"Thank you Daddy. Are you gonna take me to get my shoes?"

"You are such a teenager. No, I'm not going to be able to do that today, but I'll come get you over the weekend, okay?"

"I guess," Ladybug released an audible sigh. "Is Tracy coming?"

"It's hard to tell this early in the week, Boogie." He paused. "Do you want her to come?"

"I don't care. Well, not really."

"Why not?"

"Dad, I gotta go before I miss the bus."

As Marta listened from the kitchen, melancholy flew in the window and perched itself on her shoulder. She thought back to Ladybug's birth, the separation two years later, the transition into single-parenthood, the trauma and drama the kids experienced over the years and all the pain and hurt the photos did not capture.

"Mom, you get all the albums out every year and then you just cry and cry," Junior chuckled as he walked into the kitchen. He grabbed his bagel and took a bite. "Are you gonna keep doing this when we leave home?"

Six months shy of his eighteenth birthday, Marta pretended that his forthcoming departure for college was of little concern. With a big smile, she looked at her son and said, "Yes, I believe I will. You can bring your girlfriend to the house and I can show her all of your baby pictures."

"Mom that is not gonna happen."

Ladybug walked into the kitchen and grabbed a bagel. "Okay, I'm canceling this conversation. Come on Junior. I need to get to school on time, so I can get my celebration on!"

Junior shook his head, rolled his eyes and kissed his mother on the cheek. "Bye Mom; love you."

From the kitchen window, Marta watched her teenagers drive away in Junior's car. "Lord, I thank You for another day of life. You've seen fit to shower Your blessings upon us and I am so grateful. Thank You, Father for my two priceless jewels. I speak traveling mercies upon them. And Lord, please don't let them argue with one another in the car like they do in the house." She chuckled. "Protect them from harm. Guide them to make good choices. Let them excel in school and all that they put their hands to do." She picked up the life book, labeled "Ladybug 15" and stared at the cover.

"Father, I ask that You bless the shoe-shopping trip with Ladybug, Senior, Tracy and all the kids. Help them to have an uneventful day. No conflict, confusion or miscommunication. Just good quality time with her father and family."

Marta walked to the dining room, sat at the head of the table and opened the photo albums. The tears flowed as she turned each page of the record of their journey from pain to healing.

Home for the Holidays

By Benjamin Hicks

The bright rays beamed and highlighted every house on the street. Mr. Brown scrubbed the whitewalls on his Cadillac with his car stereo blasting. A couple of teenagers in school uniforms stood at the corner. Several neighbors sat on the concrete steps and greeted the passers by.

Moses stood in the front window and observed the morning show. Not quite nine o'clock, the temperature caused the windows to sweat. Propped between the screen and the casement, three fans blew in different directions through the living room. The front door swung open.

"Grandma, how did you meet Granddad?" Moses asked.

"We will be landing at Thurgood Marshall Airport in ten minutes," the pilot said over the loud speaker. The announcement woke Moses. After a brief tug of war for his luggage, he stood outside the airport bundled for another bitter winter. A light snow fell, as a black 2005 Nissan pulled up to the curb. Moses grabbed his luggage and threw it in the back seat.

"Thanks for picking me up, Taylor," Moses said, as he closed the car door.

"No problem. How was the flight?"

"The flight was okay, but I'm glad to be home."

"We're not home yet."

After twenty minutes of small talk, Moses said, "Pull over."

"For what?"

"I want to drive." She hesitated and then pulled the Maxima into the lot of a convenience store. "Are you serious? You're going to let me drive?"

She got out of the car and walked to the passenger side. "You just make sure you don't get a ticket."

"Whatever," he mumbled, as he scooted across the seat. He turned on the wipers to clear the accumulated snow. "It's really coming down now."

"Just be careful."

"I got this." Ten minutes later, he parked the car across the street from a dilapidated house. He got out of the car, wiped the snow off the hood and leaned on the Nissan.

"What are we doing here?" she snapped at him from inside the car.

"Welcome to heroin and crack city."

"Have you lost your mind? This is not a good area to be hanging out in the streets."

"Wait a minute."

"What are we doing here, Moses?"

He pointed to the house across the street. Tears filled his eyes. He reached into his pocket and got some tissues. Taylor jumped out the car. "Are you all right?" She rubbed his back.

"This house belonged to my grandparents. They taught me values, morals, self esteem and why God died."

"You miss them, huh?"

"With a passion."

"Let's go, Moses. I'll drive." On the way home, they passed church members evangelizing in the community.

"Look at those hypocrites," he said. He rolled down the window and yelled, "You phonies need to go home because God does not exist!"

"Moses!"

As they arrived home, they sat in the car for a few minutes. Taylor needed to tell Moses a thing or two. They got out of the car, as his mother walked onto the front porch.

"I missed you," she said, as she hugged her baby boy. Tears flowed.

"I missed you, too."

"Let me look at you." He stepped back and then spun around. "Looks like you've lost some weight. Not feeding you well at college, huh?"

"The food is okay, but nothing to write home about."

"Well, I made you some meatloaf. Want me to fix you a plate?"

"No thanks, Momma. I'm exhausted. Jet lag is a bear."

"Okay, sweetie." She tiptoed to kiss her son on the cheek. "I've turned down your bed. You get some rest."

An alarm clock and green telephone set on the nightstand next to his twin bed. The air freshener scented the room with cinnamon and pine. With his arms propped behind his head, he pondered his conversation with Taylor until sleep overtook him.

"Grandma, why are you so happy today?" Moses said, as he tugged on her blanket.

"'Cause I'm going to talk to my Lord."

"Isn't He dead?"

"No, baby." She struggled to raise her hand and ruffle his hair. "The Lord is alive and well. People act like He's not alive, but He is. Don't let anyone tell you otherwise. Now, give your grandma a hug."

The sunlight crept through the window and danced on his eyelids. The phone rang. He rubbed his eyes, reached for the phone and knocked it off the hook. "Yo cuz. How are you?"

"Who's this?"

"It's your cousin, Tyrice."

"Man, you called awful early."

"Have you been drinking? It's going on twelve." Still preoccupied with Taylor's crisis, Moses couldn't focus on the phone conversation. "Moses. Moses!"

"Huh?"

"I said, 'What are we going to do today?'"

His favorite cousin, Tyrice ran with Moses since preschool. When college separated them, emails and telephones kept them connected. The daring duo used to stay up late watching horror movies at their grandparents' house. Their house was the hot spot in the neighborhood — like the Cotton Club only instead of famous jazz musicians and singers, friends and relatives popped over. The memories caused tears to form.

"Be careful. That tone is not acceptable for my little cousin." He wiped the sleep from his eyes and sat up in the bed.

"Don't get uppity with me, college boy. We both know I run this."

"Okay, Mr. Runner." He chuckled. "Let's go to the flea market. I've got some Christmas shopping to do."

"Two weeks before, huh?"

"Yep, just like Grandma used to do."

The corner flea market housed twenty vendors with clothing, furniture, toys, food and more. For every occupied spot, two booths set empty. "Not as much activity anymore," Moses said.

"Naw, things have been pretty slow. The ghetto rats have scared off a lot of folks."

Moses noticed a rocking chair in front of the craft store. His grandmother owned a similar chair. She sat and watched the *Price Is Right* without interruption. Everyone knew not to fool with her for that hour. And if she won the showcase prize, which was more often than not, she treated the kids to candy.

She had a deep belly laugh that warmed the heart and her sense of humor and upbeat spirit kept a smile on Moses' face throughout the day. Sometimes he laughed out loud thinking about the funny things she said or did. Every Sunday morning, she sang and hummed, as she got ready for church. If her husband didn't take her to church, she grabbed her Bible and walked.

"Moses, do you remember when Granddad had us picking up cans?"

"Yes, I do. Why do you ask?"

"That older gentleman looks like him to me," he pointed toward the popcorn stand.

"Yeah, he does sort of favor Granddad."

Their grandfather was his own man. He never left home without his gun or knife tucked into the pocket of his suit jacket. Whether Sunday or Thursday, he dressed like he was going to a wedding. He loved to talk, unless the Orioles were playing, then everyone in the house had to sit quiet. His second favorite pastime was card playing. Every Saturday night, he strutted down the street to his friend's house. They played cards until the cock crowed. A faint smile spread across Moses' lips.

"Whatcha smiling about?"

"Just thinking about Granddad. He was a good guy."

"Yeah, and you're a talker just like he was."

"And?"

"Nothing. I ain't trying to get nothing started."

They picked up a few things then returned home. When Moses opened the door, his seven-year-old sister, Nicole, came out to greet him. "Hello," she said with a smile.

"Hi, Nikki." He picked her up and butterfly kissed her cheek. "Are you here by yourself?"

"No, Taylor is babysitting me."

"Well, where is she?" He put her down and looked around the room.

"She's asleep. Dad and Mom went out."

"First of all, he's not my dad. And second, you should be in bed asleep."

"Taylor said it was okay to stay up," she said with her arms crossed.

"I don't like that attitude."

"I'm going to tell on you." She ran upstairs to her room and slammed the door.

Later the next day, Moses drove through his old stomping grounds. Young boys, about grade school age, stood on the corners selling death to their own people. Screens hung from broken windows. The plywood-decorated store fronts had vulgarities spray painted on them. His eyes swelled with tears. Along with the decayed streets, his life deteriorated. He tired of the comments about him needing to polish his act. Everyone placed their faith in him as the first from his family and neighborhood to go to college. His load weighed him down and he refused to pack on anyone else's mess. He bantered with himself, as he drove through the dying area.

"College is overrated. I'm going to dropout."

"You need to save your lecture. You are preaching to the choir and the choir is singing." A lady in a tan Impala pulled up next to him. Moses pretended to adjust the radio station. "I want to have freedom to get up when I want to and do what I please." He bopped his head, as if singing to music. "No, I'm not having a mid-life crisis, I'm only twenty."

~ ~ ~ ~ ~ ~ ~

Although he and Taylor got along well now, a few years ago they were on opposite sides of enemy territory. Moses couldn't pinpoint the specific incident that started the family feud, but a truce formulated between them when they targeted a common adversary: her father.

Moses' mother dated James for a couple of years. From the beginning, Moses did not like him. Before Jim, or BJ, as he called it, Moses and his mother created a lot of fond memories together — movies, bowling, road trips to North Carolina and good conversation at the dinner table. All the good times halted when James entered the scene. Fellowship at dinnertime was more like a one-monk monastery. Looking at James made him nauseous, especially at mealtime, so Moses often ate alone.

Not bold enough to challenge him physically, James taunted Moses with words. For nights on end, he insulted and assaulted his character and molding manhood. When Moses spoke to defend himself, his mother intervened. He spent many nights letting the sun go down on his wrath. When James moved his daughter in, she too landed on the receiving end of the verbal abuse.

One Saturday night before Moses left for college, he heard his mother crying. He walked into the kitchen. "Mom! What happened?"

"Oh, oh. I uh, fell down the porch steps." She tried to stand, but plopped back on the chair. Moses ran to help her.

"Ma, you didn't fall down those steps. What happened?"

"Nothing." She pulled her arm away from him. "I'm okay. Just get me some ice."

He ran to the refrigerator and filled a baggie with ice. He wrapped it in a clean dishcloth and placed it on her eye.

"Did James hit you?"

"Now Moses, you know how I can talk. I said something I shouldn't have and he corrected me for it."

"Excuse me? He corrected you for it?" What kind of —"

"You let me handle this."

"Handle it? Handle it?! You're not doing a very good job of handling it. Look at your face!" He helped his mother to the mirror hanging over the living room couch. When she saw the hues of purple and black that circled her left eye, she cried.

"It's my fault. I keep —"

"This is not your fault Momma."

A couple hours later, when the lock unlatched, Moses reached behind the living room couch. With bat in hand, he positioned himself to hit a homerun.

"Moses, what are you doing?" His mother stepped between him and home base. "Boy, put that bat down."

James walked in the house, "What's going on?"

"Why have you been beating my mother?" Moses smushed his mother between himself and the enemy. Tipsy from his late-night festivities, James cocked his head to the right. Taylor and Nikki had crept downstairs and stood on the bottom step.

"What are you doing to my daddy?" Nikki asked.

"Your daddy has been beating our momma and now I'm going to beat him." He raised the bat. "Now go to bed and close the door."

Nikki ran to the phone and dialed 911. Taylor grabbed her stepbrother. "Come on Moses. Don't do this. You'll end up in jail and we'll be stuck here with him." She sneered at her father and then said, "Mrs. Jones, take him on the porch to cool off."

"I don't wanna coo-cool off." He tried to resist, but the Cold Duck got the best of him. About half James' weight, she pulled him outside and sat him on the stoop.

"How long has he been beating my momma?" Tears streamed down his face as he puffed his cheeks.

"For a while now. That's why I taught Nikki to dial 911."

"Why didn't you tell me?"

The police arrived ten minutes later and questioned everyone. "Ma'am, do you want to press charges?"

"No." She grabbed the couch pillow and hugged it like a teddy bear.

"No! What do you mean 'No?' Look what he did to her!" Moses shook his head.

"I-I promise I will never hit you again, baby." James stroked his wife's face. "I'm so sorry."

"It's okay," she clutched the pillow tighter.

The officer turned to Moses. "I'm sorry sir, but you'll have to leave. She doesn't want to press charges and you were the aggressor."

"I'm out." Moses stormed out the house and slammed the door.

~ ~ ~ ~ ~ ~ ~

When Moses returned home from his spin around the desolate community, he heard his mother and Taylor whispering in the dining room.

"What's going on here?"

"Shhhh," Taylor motioned for him to come closer.

"I've decided to leave James," his mother said.

"Woo hoo!"

"Shhhhh," Taylor threw her index finger to her lips. "He's upstairs."

"Woo hoo," he whispered, with a grin as wide as the Baltimore Harbor. The last ten years had been a nightmare for him and he found it hard to contain his excitement. Rolaids didn't spell relief, divorce did. He shimmied around the kitchen.

"Could you show a little more excitement?"

"Sorry, Mom. I know this was a tough decision, but you do deserve better." He rubbed his mother's back. "I'm more concerned about how Nikki will take it." Moses recalled the anguish he experienced when his mother and father divorced. For two years, he suffered from sleepless nights, anxiety attacks and loss of appetite. He hoped Nikki's gentle soul didn't become a hurting soul like him.

~ ~ ~ ~ ~ ~ ~ ~

Six more shopping days. No need to turn on the radio because the only music that blasted on the stations was Gospel. In preparation for the NBA game coming on in an hour, he fixed himself a sandwich and chips. Nikki and his mother walked downstairs flaunting mother-daughter dresses with hats, shoes and purses to match.

"Mom, where are you two going?"

"We're going to church. Do you want to go?"

"Nope."

"Are you coming to my piano solo next Sunday?" Nikki pretended to work the ivory keys.

"Nope." Moses loved his little sister, but he could not bring himself to go to that church. The saints prayed for him to come back, but he had no interest in returning. He acknowledged that God allowed him to make it to his junior year in college, but he had no desire to praise Him for it. His blessing of higher education had morphed into a curse.

The next day, Moses researched home-based businesses at the local library. Drawn away from the heap of books in front of him, he noticed an attractive young lady in the next aisle. She looked his way and smiled — a love ballad that sang to his heart. He blushed. By the time he gathered enough nerve to approach her, she was gone. Bummer. He spent a couple more hours researching and then headed for the checkout desk. He gave the librarian his library card.

"Excuse me, you dropped this," the fleeting damsel handed him a piece of paper. Moses took it. "You're welcome."

"Excuse my manners. Your words left me speechless and I forgot my name." She laughed. The librarian returned his card. "I'm Moses." He stuffed the card in his back pocket and grabbed his books. "And you are?"

"You'll know the next time we meet." She waved and walked away.

Back at home the library books were sprawled over the kitchen table.

"Moses, come to the kitchen!" His mother said.

"Mom, I'm in the bathroom."

"When you finish what you're doing, come to the kitchen."

As he bounced down the stairs and walked into the kitchen, his mother fanned papers in her hand. "What is all this?"

"Look Mom I —"

"Don't look Mom me. You've only got a year left. I didn't work two jobs to send you to college for you to dropout. I'm not having that." She threw his papers on the table.

"Mom, I already made my decision."

"Then you won't be living here." His mother marched away, as James entered the kitchen. Moses gathered his things and proceeded to his room. He bumped into Taylor on the stairs.

"When are you going to tell him?" he said to his sister.

"That's where I'm headed now."

"Want me to stick around?"

"No, I'm good. Thanks." Moses sat on the stairs as Taylor tried to talk to her dad. He gave her the I'm-too-busy speech again. They heard it so many times Moses figured she mouthed the words with him.

~ ~ ~ ~ ~ ~ ~

143

Delving into his research, Moses returned to the library. To his surprise, he ran into the young lady. Blinded by her brilliance at their first encounter, he didn't realize that she worked at the library. On her break, she sat with him.

"Hi, Moses."

"Hi. Hey, how'd you know my name?"

"You told me."

"Oh yeah." He took a deep breath and then continued. "So are you going to tell me your name today?"

"Virginia."

"Hi, Virginia. Got any plans for Thursday?"

"Man, you sure move quick." She grabbed a pen and scribbled on a piece of paper. "Here's my number and address. How about Thursday at eight?"

"Works for me. I'll see you Thursday."

With only a day to get ready, Moses jogged home with books in tow. He ran to his room and snatched a couple suits out of the closet. He scrambled to his dresser to find matching socks. *Things are looking up.*

Cussing and fussing interrupted his thoughts. Taylor and her father were engaged in a heated argument. As he ran down the hall, someone knocked on the front door. The police. Nikki must have called them. They separated the quarrelers and gave them both warnings. James learned that he had five months to prepare for grandpa-ism and he didn't take the news too well.

On Thursday, Moses stepped out of GQ and into his mother's room. Her mouth dropped.

"Now young man, where are you going?" She straightened his tie. "I know you are not going to church."

"Not at all, Mom. I'm going out on a date."

"Who's the lucky lady?"

"Someone that I've been talking to."

"You be safe," she said, as she hugged him.

He pulled up to the address Virginia had jotted down for him. A lot of young people, dressed for success, walked into the church. A sign outside the building read "Revival."

"This can't be the right address." He double-checked the note and then noticed Virginia waving at him from the parking lot. "This can't be."

She walked to the car. "Why are you just sitting in the car?"

"I can't do this. I'm sorry."

"Why not?"

"I just can't face the Lord and the church right now. Let's go somewhere else."

"I can't do that."

"Okay, I'm out of here. Bye." The tires screeched as he drove away.

Christmas was three days away. Carolers strolled the neighborhood admiring the festive lights and spreading joy through songs. Kids made snow forts and attacked each other with ice bombs. Moses peered down at the happy holiday folks from his bedroom window. "God, why are You trying to mess up my Christmas?" Moses asked.

"I'll get it," Taylor chimed as she opened the front door. "Moses, you have company." Not expecting any visitors, he took his time getting downstairs.

"Hello, Moses," Virginia said, as she smiled.

"I'll leave you two alone," Taylor disappeared up the stairs.

"I had to see you. I felt bad about the other night. I got your address from the library database. I hope you don't mind."

"Don't worry about it." He escorted her to the dining room and pulled the chair out for her. "Would you like something to drink?"

"A glass of water, please."

Moses' mother came into the room. "Mom, this is my friend, Virginia." Virginia stood and the ladies shook hands.

"Nice to meet you, Virginia."

"Thank you. Likewise," she said, as she took her seat next to Moses.

"Moses, your sisters and I are going out to get something to eat. Do you and Virginia want anything? My treat."

They looked at each other and said, "Sure."

With the house empty, Virginia dug a little deeper. "What is your beef with the church?"

Moses squirmed in his seat. "Nothing."

"It has to be something because you were buggin' out the other day."

"Just wait a minute. Who are you judging?"

"Look, I like you, and I know you like me."

"True."

"But my first love is the Lord. And you need to know that light and darkness cannot be together."

"I used to be in love with the Lord," he paused to compose himself. "Until both my grandparents died of cancer. God took them away when He could have saved them. So, since He turned His back on me, I turned mine on Him."

"So is Christmas a regular day for you?"

"Yeah, in the sense of not giving Him any joy for the holiday. I give my grandparents the joy by honoring their tradition."

"You are truly a lost soul. You remind me of Saul. His name changed to Paul when he saw the light."

"My light has been put out."

"I'll be praying for you." She touched his hand. "In the meantime, draw from the strength of your name, Moses. In the Bible, Moses was a doubter, but what did he do? He led God's people to the Promised Land. It took him a long time, but he did it with God's guidance."

~ ~ ~ ~ ~ ~ ~

Nikki ran into Moses' room and jumped on his bed. "It's Christmas time!" He pulled the covers over his head. She yanked them off the bed, then screamed in his ear, "It's Christmas — time to get up and open the gifts."

Moses rolled out of bed and plopped on the floor. Nikki grabbed his hand and pulled him. "Come on slow poke." He picked up Nikki and propped her on his shoulders. They hopped to the Christmas tree.

"Where is the man of the house?" Sarcasm bounced off Taylor's lips.

"When you see the man of the house, let me know," Moses said as Nikki slid down his back to the floor. "Just getting in I see?"

"Mind your business."

"You two need to stop that," his mother said.

Nikki ripped through the gift-wrapping. After they opened the presents, the ladies decided to go to church, Taylor included. On their way out the door, his mother handed him an envelope.

"What's this?"

"A letter from your grandmother," she said as she adjusted Nikki's dress.

"You've had this letter all these years? Why give it to me now?"

"It's time." The group departed and he opened the letter.

"Dear Precious,

If you are reading this letter, I'm gone to a better place. Don't cry for me because God has a plan for me. Don't blame your mother or God for my death. We all have to go sometime, but it's how you go and where you go that's important. Life sometimes leaves us alone, but that is when we must rededicate our life to Him. You see Precious, God can't be taken away from us. You decide whether you want Him in your life. He doesn't force Himself on you. Many people doubt His name, but they can't doubt the miracles that He blessed us to see and have.

Stormy weather will come, but don't let the storms keep you from your blessings. I truly believe God has something around the corner for you, but you have to be patient. Study your Word. That gives you strength and inspiration when life gets you down. It's a cold world, but the church is your shelter. Prayer can make a difference, I know. Dry those tears. Love and respect your mother. Stop holding yourself back and reach for the stars. And always seek God's guidance. I'm proud of you. I was there when you received your acceptance letter to college and know that I will be there when you graduate. My baby will have a degree. I'm so proud of you. My love is always with you, no matter what you are going through.

Love always,
Grandma"

~ ~ ~ ~ ~ ~ ~

The church was filled to capacity. The choir, donned in purple and white robes, sang *I Am God*. The presence of the Lord filled the sanctuary. The door swung open and in walked Moses. As he looked for his family, he heard a several people thank God for his return. His little sister ran and jumped in his arms. Moses rededicated his life to the Lord. His mother was overjoyed all day, even though her husband never came home

148

that night. She left all her drama at the altar like he did. He felt different, but in a good way. The weight of the world lifted off his shoulders.

~ ~ ~ ~ ~ ~ ~

Two years later, his mother started a healing ministry to help people cope with divorce. She went back to graduate school to complete her theology degree. Nikki had some turbulent times trying to adjust, but prayer, counseling and regular visits with James, smoothed her transition. In the fifth grade, and growing an inch almost daily, she prefers to be addressed as Nicole.

Taylor named her son Eugene and married his father in June. Moses graduated from college and is a deacon in the church. He and his wife, Virginia, are pursuing master's degrees in accounting. They have a small business that handles income tax returns for many of the city's churches. When God blesses you, He blesses you.

Daddy's Girls

A short story by Michelle Larks

Chapter One

Sydney Morris walked into her thirteen-year-old daughter's bedroom. "Tina, have you finished packing your bag yet?" Tina sat slumped on her bed, head bowed. "Your father will be here any minute to pick you up."

"Almost," Tina answered sullenly. "Mom, do you know where my red sweater is?" A reed-thin, late-blooming teenager, Tina took after her sire in height and complexion. Barefoot, she stood five-feet ten-inches and had at least five more years of growth. Much to Tina's chagrin, she towered over most of her classmates, boys and girls. She felt clumsy around the shorter, curvier girls. A bad case of acne had lowered the young girl's shaky self-esteem. Tina wished she were more like her mother. Petite with a flawless complexion, a short brown bob adorned her attractive oval face.

"Oops, I knew there was something I meant to do," Sydney answered, smacking her forehead exasperated. She walked to her room. "Your top is still at the cleaners. I meant to get the clothes today."

"I don't have anything to wear," Tina tossed her bag on the bed. "Dang, when I forget something she has a fit," she muttered under her breath.

"Did you say something young lady?" Sydney's voice rose.

Does she have super hearing or something? "No ma'am. I just don't have anything to wear. Can I stay home?" Tina opened the closet door to look for something to take in place of the sweater. She searched inside the closet, pushing hangers from side to side.

"No, staying home is not an option." Sydney slid open her dresser drawer to look for an outing outfit. She had planned a ladies night out with her girlfriends, Kimberly and Rene. Employed as a help desk technician, her workweek had been long and arduous.

"Michael is looking forward to you staying with him and Eva this weekend. He's been busy with the baby and you two haven't gotten together in a long time." She walked into her daughter's room.

Tina sat hunched on the edge of the bed, gnawing her fingernails. Her dark brown hair was bunched into a white scrunchy. One stray lock dangled over her wide forehead. Dressed in her usual uniform, blue jeans and an old oversized blue and white plaid flannel shirt that belonged to her father, she covered her feet with Timberland boots.

Tina's room was somewhat messy. Posters of her favorite music artists covered one wall. Barbie, Cabbage Patch and American Girl dolls aligned the side of her bed next to the other wall — childhood toys that Tina now disdained as babyish.

Sydney sighed and panned the room. "Do you think you'll have time to straighten this pig sty before your dad comes to pick you up?"

"I would have if someone hadn't forgotten my sweater." She flinched as she remembered to whom she was speaking. "I'm still trying to figure out what I'm going to wear tomorrow. Want to give me money to buy something new?" Tina batted her eyes.

"I don't think so. I'll give you money to get your sweater out of the cleaners. That's it."

"Mommy that's not fair. Why do I have to suffer because you forgot to do something?" Tina stood and packed her folded clothing into the oversized duffle bag on her bed.

Sydney picked up the comb, brush and scrunchies on Tina's dresser and put them into the bag. She turned and hugged her daughter. "It's called life. Everyone forgets to do something, sometimes." She tugged Tina's hair. "Bear with me. I'm sure your dad won't have a problem stopping at the cleaners on the way to his house. I'm going to get the ticket and some money. Voila, your problem is solved."

"Do I have to go to Daddy's?" She tossed a couple more items into the bag and flopped onto the bed. "I don't want to. Mommy, please don't make me go." Her countenance crumpled, as a tear trickled down her face.

Sydney walked back into the room and held her daughter. "I know the divorce and your father's remarrying has been a big adjustment for you. Remember when we talked to your therapist? We agreed that you should visit your dad a few times and see how things work out."

"I hate Cheyenne. What kind of name is that anyway?" She slapped the bed. "I hate Daddy for leaving us and having a baby with another woman."

Tina's outburst was a repetitious refrain expressed since her father announced Eva was expecting. Though her parents had been divorced for seven years, she had not come to terms with his new wife and daughter. When Eva gave birth to his second child eight months ago, their relationship hit a rough patch. Tina's jealousy ignited refusal to see her baby sister. Her parents prayed that today would be the onset of a breakthrough.

The doorbell chimed. "That's probably your father. I'll get the door." She patted Tina's arm and headed out the bedroom. "I want you to finish packing, young lady."

"Hi, Sydney. Is Tina ready to go?"

Sydney checked the mailbox and motioned her ex-husband inside. Michael sprawled his muscular girth on the couch in the living room. Not drop-dead gorgeous, but easy on the eyes. His face was spotted with healed blemishes. His brown eyes crinkled to small slits when he laughed.

After picking up a letter that fluttered to the floor, Sydney walked to the chair across from her ex-husband. Wearing her favorite purple fleece jogging suit, she sat Indian style in the plush chair.

"Tina is feeling apprehensive about spending the weekend with you and Eva. She's been balking and giving me excuses about why she should stay home." She placed the mail on the end table. "I think we should follow Dr. Duvall's advice and give her visit a try, regardless of all the attitude."

Michael grunted and looked at Sydney. Guilt riddled his face. "You're right. I didn't think it would be this difficult to maintain a relationship with my daughter. Tina has always been my girl. She's my princess."

Sydney nodded. "Just keep reassuring her that she's your girl. She'll be all right. How's the baby?"

Michael's face split in a wide grin. "Cheyenne is doing great. She reminds me of Tina when she was a baby."

Tina walked into the room with the duffle bag slung across her shoulder. "Hi, Daddy."

Michael jumped from the couch. "How are you doing, Princess? I've been waiting all week for Friday, so I can spend the weekend with you." He buzzed her cheek. She rolled her eyes at him and then burst into giggles.

As Sydney watched her ex-husband and daughter, her heart ached. At times, she wanted to blink like Barbara Eden of *I*

Dream of Jeannie and magically restore her family. Life was simple a few years ago.

"Eva is looking forward to you spending the weekend with us." He tickled Tina. "We're going out to dinner tomorrow and she mentioned taking you to the mall." He reached for the duffle bag.

Tina sucked her teeth and rolled her eyes. She shot her mother an SOS look. Sydney nodded encouragingly. She walked to Tina and hugged her.

"You have my cell number. Use it if I'm not home," she whispered. "Call me this weekend, if you want to talk. Michael is still your father and he loves you, no matter how many other children he has." She kissed her baby girl on the cheek. "Try to have a good time."

Tina slipped on her sky blue University of North Carolina Tarheels Starter jacket. Hesitating, she followed her father out the door. Sydney scurried to her room to find something to wear. She glanced at her watch. In a few hours, she would be unwinding with her girlfriends.

Chapter Two

The evening moved at a snail's pace. Dinner had been a disaster. Eva ordered a large sausage and cheese pizza for dinner, unaware that Tina did not eat pork. She winced every time Tina removed a piece of meat from her food.

"How is school coming along?" Eva asked, trying to put her stepdaughter at ease.

"Okay." Tina plopped a chunk of sausage on the napkin. Before the divorce, Friday nights were basketball nights — a weekly ritual reserved for herself and her father.

When they retired to the family room, Eva sat between them on the couch. Her presence created a physical wedge between father and daughter. Tina unceremoniously rose from the couch and sat on the floor. Sesame Street boomed on the high definition television.

"Did I tell you that I was a cheerleader in high school?" Eva asked. She cradled Cheyenne in her arms and motioned for Tina to hold her.

"Really," Tina kept her attention glued to the television screen and refused to acknowledge Eva or her sister.

Michael had taken Tina on a tour of his new house in Richton Park earlier that evening. She noted the Cheyenne shrine. Hundreds of framed pictures were scattered about the house. An altar was erected in Cheyenne's honor in the master suite. Tina shrugged. Not one picture of herself.

"I've been working a lot of overtime lately," he said, as he noticed her reaction. "I needed more money for the new house, the baby and your child support. I just haven't gotten around to putting your pictures up yet." He rubbed her back. "Maybe we can do that together this weekend."

Tina nodded and forced a smile. *Do I even exist in his world?*

From the family room couch, Eva made another failed attempt to build a bond between the sisters. "Would you like to hold Cheyenne?"

Tina looked at the sprouted horns atop her stepmother's head. "Nope, I don't like babies. All they do is cry and puke."

Cheyenne chortled. Her chubby arms reached for Michael. He took the baby from Eva just as the telephone rang. "I'll get it," Eva said, grateful to make an exit from the room.

From the corner of her eye, Tina watched her father play with the baby. A lump rose in her throat and goose bumps raced down her back. *I bet he used to play with me like that.* "I wonder what Mommy is doing."

He peered at her and then shook his head. "Hmm, I don't know."

"Maybe she has a date," Tina said, trying to get a rise out of her father.

"If she does, that's good," he tossed Cheyenne in the air. "Your mother is an attractive woman. I'm sure she has to fight off men all the time."

Worry settled on her face like Bell's palsy. What if her mother was out with a man? She never told Tina her plans for the evening. "Maybe I should call and check on her."

"No, let her enjoy herself."

~ ~ ~ ~ ~ ~ ~

Sydney sat in the paneled basement of Rene's house, sipping a virgin strawberry daiquiri. Tonya Baker's *Life In Him* streamed from the CD player. The friends had just devoured rotisserie chicken, tossed salad and twice-baked potatoes. Rene, a cute woman with high cheekbones, wore a mop of curly auburn hair. She took off her glasses, laid them on the cocktail table and flopped on the sofa.

Kimberly, the last of the trio, lounged in the leather recliner. She snapped her fingers to the music and then sipped her sparkling grape juice. Kimberly was a full-figured girl. Her short hair was twisted and dimples wreathed her face. The ladies had been friends since high school.

"I'm surprised Tina hasn't called you yet," Kimberly said.

"Me, too. I hope things are going well for her." Sydney reached for the remote. "She hasn't spent a weekend at Michael's in awhile."

"That's a shame," Rene interjected. "Just because of the new wifey and baby. I never imagined Michael would neglect his child." She popped a potato chip in her mouth.

"I wouldn't call it neglect. Tina is jealous of Eva. By the time she semi-adjusted to her stepmother's presence, Eva was pregnant. That's really when the problems started." She surfed the channels for a repeat of *Law & Order*. "Girl, when Tina refused to go to Michael's house, I thought I would pull my hair out. The job had me running crazy. And instead of Tina going to Michael's every other weekend, I had to cope with her being in the house." She placed her hands on her hips and mimicked her sassy daughter. "With that I-know-everything attitude," her hands dropped to her side, as shame jumped on her back. "I guess I didn't handle the situation too well."

"We know it's difficult raising her alone," Rene said. "At least you took her to counseling. Think of all the children who don't have that luxury."

"Too bad Eva didn't have a boy," Kimberly said, as she leaned back in the recliner. "At least Tina would still be Michael's only girl."

"Truthfully, I don't think that would have made a difference. Tina would have acted the same regardless of the baby's gender. It doesn't help that Eva is a lot younger than us either. I think that's part of the problem. She's too young to cope with a teenage stepdaughter." Sydney's eyes misted. "I wish Momma was still alive. When she passed, my life fell apart." She brushed a tear from the corner of her eye.

Rene stood and walked to Sydney. She rubbed her shoulder. "We probably could have done a little more to help you cope when things got rough, but we thought Michael had your back. We never imagined you and Michael would break up after Ms. Pat passed."

Patricia Williams, Sydney's mother, had been diagnosed with leukemia. Her illness took a huge toll on Sydney and her marriage. Sydney was unable to cope with her mother's illness and subsequent death. As an only child, she lost a huge chunk of her heart when her mother died. She neglected Michael and Tina and became indifferent to life.

Michael knew the bond between mother and daughter was strong. He knew that Sydney needed time to come to terms with her mother's death. However, he did not anticipate her apparent cessation of love for him. She refused to share her feelings and their home life took a nosedive. At her manager's suggestion, Sydney took a leave of absence.

When Michael left for work, Sydney lay huddled under the covers, sniffing quietly. When he returned, Sydney was still in bed. A howling, hungry and smelly Tina greeted him at the threshold of the filthy house. Arguments erupted and continued nonstop. His last ditch effort to snap his wife out of her grief was a month-long sabbatical. He took Tina and stayed with his sister in the suburbs.

After Michael left with Tina, Sydney's despair increased. Abandoned by her true love, she fell into a catatonic state. By the grace of God, Rene and Kimberly ministered to her hurt. Rene, the single one of the group, moved in with her friend. After much prayer, fasting and fellowship, Sydney regained her sanity and walked the road to recovery.

On the weekends, Kimberly relieved Rene and took Sydney to her house. Married with two sons, Kimberly opened her home to her mother several years earlier. Mema was instrumental in Sydney's recovery.

By the time Sydney showed signs of life, Michael was done with the marriage. He did not know what spurred Sydney back to life, but too much had been said and done between them. He never returned home. He sued Sydney for divorce and requested joint custody of Tina.

"I don't know what I'd do without your support." Sydney said. "I love you both."

"Girl, you ain't said nothing but a word. You'd do the same for us. That's what friends are for."

"When I look back at Momma's illness, it seems like a dream. I never imagined life without my mother. I felt alone, even though I had Michael and Tina. My family just never seemed complete without her." She rubbed her hands together to wipe away the Orville Redenbacher butter.

"We talked to each other on the telephone every day. She knew that life wasn't going to be easy for me without her and she tried to prepare me. But there's nothing you can do to fill the void of a mother's love." She pulled her friends in for a group hug. "I can't thank you two enough for being there for me." She paused. "Enough about me. What movies did you get for us to watch this week?"

Rene grinned at her friends. "What would ladies night be without a good Denzel movie? I rented *Out of Time* and *Why Do Fools Fall in Love?*. That little Larenz Tate is a cutie."

Kimberly stood, "I'm going to put some more popcorn in the microwave. Anyone want something else to drink? Let's get this party started."

Chapter Three

Tina awakened to loud cries that punctured the air. *Dang, a person can't sleep around here with all that noise. I wish I was at home.* She put the floral pillow over her head to muffle the sobs. The door to Michael and Eva's bedroom opened. Tina heard footsteps on the hardwood floors. She picked up the remote control and turned on the television. After an eternity of wailing, Cheyenne stopped crying. Tina changed the channels, until she settled on a *That's So Raven* rerun on Nickelodeon. Critical, she looked around the room.

"This will be your room," her father promised, when she last stayed with him. The dark furniture had water rings, nicks and missing handles. Rummage sale reject. Tina lay in her twin bed with the Dora the Explorer comforter. A dresser and chest of drawers set on opposing empty walls. Barren.

Someone knocked on her bedroom door. *I hope that's not Eva.* "Come in," Tina said.

Her father walked into the room. Clad in striped pajamas, he carried Cheyenne. She sucked from the Winnie-the-Pooh bottle clutched in her balled hands. "I just wanted to see if you were up. Eva's fixing breakfast. It should be ready in about twenty minutes." Cheyenne squealed with excitement, when she saw Tina. She dropped the bottle and cooed.

Tina sat up on the bed and pushed her hair away from her face. "I'm up. I just hadn't gotten out of the bed yet." She stretched for a full body yawn. "What is Eva making for breakfast? I hope something better than the pizza we had for dinner last." She ignored Cheyenne.

"I should have told Eva you didn't like meat. That was my fault. Give her a chance Tina. She's good people." He picked up the bottle. "After breakfast, Eva wants to take you to the mall. I'm going to stay home with the baby. Spending the day with Eva will give you two time to get to know each other better."

"I don't want to go to the mall with just her. Why can't you come with us Daddy?" Tina folded her arms across her chest and poked out her lips.

"Because I want two of my most favorite girls in the world to get to know each other better. You don't have the option of staying home, or of me going with you. We can plan a family outing the next time you stay over."

"But we're not a family anymore. Eva and Cheyenne are your family. Mom is mine."

"That's not true. You have two families. One includes your mother and the other one consists of me, Eva and Cheyenne. Now get up and get dressed so we can eat. You'll enjoy yourself at the mall. Eva loves shopping almost as much as you do." He turned to leave the room. Cheyenne stared at Tina wide-eyed. Tina stuck out her tongue, crossed her eyes and used her hands to flap moose ears.

Tina showered. She put on a pair of black jeans, a white turtleneck shell and a white and black plaid shirt. She fluffed and sprayed her hair, then sauntered into the kitchen.

"Good morning." Eva put the dishes on the dishwasher rack in the cabinet. "Did you sleep well?"

"Yeah, I slept okay." Tina slid into an empty chair at the oak kitchen table. "Where's Daddy?"

"His job called. There was an emergency at work and he had to go in." She grabbed a plate from the cabinet. "He told me to tell you that he'll be home as soon as he can, so that we can still go to the mall."

A pang of fear shot through Tina. She cringed. Home alone with Eva.

Eva handed her a plate of scrambled eggs and a piece of toast. "There's grape and strawberry jam on the table."

Tina preferred her eggs cooked sunny side up, but after last night's dinner fiasco, she decided to let the issue go.

Eva finished putting the dishes in the cabinet and re-loaded the dishwasher. A bottle of milk was heating atop the stove.

Eva wiped her hands on the dishtowel and laid it on the white and black counter. "I'm going to give Cheyenne another bottle. She's been a little fussy this morning. After she goes to sleep, maybe we can sit and talk."

Tina kept eating. She wolfed down the food, laid her soiled plate in the sink, rushed back to the bedroom and quietly locked the door. She turned on the television, curled into a ball and fell asleep.

~ ~ ~ ~ ~ ~ ~

Jolted awake, Tina heard Cheyenne screaming as if someone was throttling her. She sat up on the bed and shook her head. Tina grabbed a magazine out of her duffle bag. She read a couple of paragraphs and then saw the telephone on the nightstand. She dialed her home number.

"Hi, Mommy. How are you?" Tina twisted the telephone cord between her fingers.

"I'm fine, baby. How is my favorite girl?" Sydney was in the middle of dusting the furniture in the living room. She dropped the rag on the floor and sat on the sofa.

"Okay. Daddy had to go to work and I'm here with Eva and the baby."

"That's nice. You need to spend some time with your sister." Sydney had the phone propped between her neck and shoulder, as she straightened the pile of magazines on the bottom shelf of the cocktail table.

"She's not my sister. She's my Daddy's baby."

"I don't care how you want to categorize Cheyenne; she is still your sister."

"Half-sister." Tina corrected her mother. "Anyway, she's been screaming her head off all day. I can't get any rest."

"Maybe she's not feeling well." Sydney's black slippers dangled from her feet.

"Whatever. I wish Daddy were here so he could bring me home. I don't like it here."

"You only have one more day. Besides, since your dad had to work today, you didn't get to spend a lot of time with him. I'm sure he'll make up for it tomorrow."

"We had pizza for dinner yesterday and Eva ordered it with sausage," Tina scraped her tongue along the roof of her mouth. "I had to pick the meat out. It was yucky. I can still taste it." Cheyenne screamed again. "See what I mean," Tina sat crossly. "I can't get any rest. All that noise is getting on my nerves. I gotta go Mom. Eva's knocking at the door." Tina quietly hung up the telephone. She stood and opened the door.

With her hair frazzled and her eyes shrouded with dark circles, Eva waved her left hand erratically and cupped Cheyenne in her right. "I just got off the phone with the pediatrician. He thinks she has an ear infection. I need to go to Walgreen's and pick up antibiotics for her." She offered the baby to Tina. "Would you keep an eye on Cheyenne until I come back?"

"Me? I don't know anything about babies. Can't you take her with you?" Tina looked up at the ceiling, then back at Eva. "I tell you what, I can hold her while you drive and go in the store." Tina's eyes were wide as saucers. She did not want any part of taking care of Cheyenne.

"It's too chilly outside," Eva said apologetically. "The wind will irritate her even more. I won't be gone long. No more than twenty minutes."

"I guess so. What do you want me to do?" Tina rubbed her hands on the side of her pants.

"Follow me." Eva placed Cheyenne in her crib and then ran downstairs. Tina hustled to keep up and almost lost her footing. Eva slipped on a brown jacket from the closet. "I'll hurry. I don't want Cheyenne to suffer any more than she has to." She closed the door behind her.

Tina locked the door. She sat on the sofa, praying Cheyenne would stay asleep, or whatever it was she was doing until Eva returned. Tina glanced fearfully toward the baby's room. Attentive, Tina sat in silence for about five minutes. She heard Cheyenne whimpering. Soon the baby worked herself into a full crying jag. Tina ignored Cheyenne for a few minutes, but the baby continued to howl.

Tina stood timidly and tiptoed into the room. Cheyenne lay on her back. Her little legs, clad in pink pajamas, flailed in the air. Her hand was firmly clasped over her left ear. The baby caught sight of Tina, who stared petrified. Cheyenne gulped and screamed again. Tina inched closer to the bed. She patted Cheyenne's head. The baby continued to sob until her voice became hoarse. The howling hurt Tina's ears. She looked toward the doorway and shut her eyes tight. She put her hands over her ears, as if willing Eva to magically appear. Tina turned her attention back to the wailing infant. She picked up Cheyenne, held her in her arms and bounced her gently.

Carrying the squirming, crying baby, Tina took a deep breath and walked into the living room. She sat on the sofa. Tina held Cheyenne's arm in her hand and peered into the baby's face. Though her face was contorted and red from crying, Tina was stunned to see how much Cheyenne resembled her. The sisters had their father's nose and lips. Tina patted Cheyenne's damp, matted hair.

Cheyenne gulped, cried and then made choking, wheezing noises. Tina clutched her sister close to her thin chest. "Don't cry, Cheyenne. Your mommy will be back in a minute." She rocked her anguished sibling. "She's coming back with medicine that will make you feel better. I know. I used to take the pink stuff myself."

Tina's face blanched. She almost dropped the baby. Cheyenne wasn't breathing. She softly shook the child. *Oh my God. What am I going to do?* She stared at Cheyenne's chest hypnotically, but could not detect any movement. Tears trickled from the corners of Cheyenne's eyes. Tina laid the baby's limp body on the couch and knelt on the floor in front of her.

"Lord, help me remember how to do CPR." Tina's hands shook, as she placed her mouth over Cheyenne's little nostrils and mouth and exhaled. She stopped and repeated her ministrations several more times. Sweat flew as she flung the hair out of her face. Just as the baby whimpered and expelled a weak cry, Tina detected movement behind her.

"What's going on?" her father asked as he ran to his daughters. Eva was two steps behind him with medicine in hand.

"She quit breathing Daddy. I —"

"Call 911," he yelled to Eva and picked up Cheyenne. Tina crumpled to the floor and bawled.

Eva rushed to the kitchen and made the call. Michael took Cheyenne into the kitchen. "What were you thinking?" He paced the floor cradling his baby.

"I thought it'd be better for Cheyenne if I didn't take her outside." She hung up the phone. "I wasn't gone long."

"Yeah, well we'll have to finish this conversation later." He gave Cheyenne to her mother. "I've got to check on Tina."

He returned to the living room, knelt on the floor and gathered her shaking body in his arms. "You did good Princess. You saved the baby's life."

Chapter Four

The ambulance siren wailed. The red and white truck transporting Eva and Cheyenne to the hospital whipped around the corner. Michael and Tina followed in the mint green, Dodge mini-van. Tina held her father's right hand like it was a brand new Baby Phat purse.

"Is Cheyenne going to be okay Daddy?" She cleared the lump in her throat. "I was so scared when she stopped breathing and turned blue. For a minute I froze, then remembered what I learned in the CPR class Momma made me take. Who would have thought I'd actually have to use it? And on my sister."

Her comment touched Michael's heart. Although he had prayed for a less dramatic resolve, the events of the evening were the catalyst to bridge the gap between him and his princesses. "I'm sure she'll be fine." He pulled the car in the emergency room parking lot. "I'm glad your mother made you take the classes, too."

He locked the door with the remote as they sprinted into the hospital. Eva stood at the in-take station. She opened her purse and handed the nurse her medical insurance card.

Tina sat in the middle row of chairs. She wished she had a cell phone so she could call her mother. *To think I didn't like my own sister. She's only a baby.*

Eva sidled through the row. She sat next to Tina and hugged her stepdaughter. "Thank you so much for reviving Cheyenne." Eva's voice trembled. Her moist eyes drooped exhaustedly. "The EMT operators said that you did a great job of taking care of Cheyenne. I don't know if I would have been able to do what you did."

"It was nothing," Tina said. With a coy expression, she twiddled her thumbs.

"I wanted to thank you again." She stood and closed her purse. "I'm going back to the room with Cheyenne."

"Do you mind if I go with Eva?" her father asked. "Or do you want me to stay with you?"

"Go ahead, Daddy." She waved him on to follow Eva. "But could I use your cell phone? I want to call Mom."

He tossed her the phone. "Sure, Princess. I'll be with Eva and Cheyenne."

Tina strolled outside the building as she dialed her house. The telephone rang five times, then routed to voice mail. She pressed the disconnect button and dialed her mother's cell phone number. "Mom, you'll never guess what happened."

Sydney listened with her mouth gaped open. Her eyes grew wide as eggs. "Oh baby, I know you were scared out of your mind. I'm so proud of you. How is Cheyenne doing?"

"Daddy and Eva are in the emergency room with her now." She sat on the bench. "You're right, Mom. I was afraid Cheyenne wouldn't start breathing again. I thought about calling the hospital first, but she got sick so fast."

"Where were Michael and Eva when Cheyenne got sick?" Sydney ran her hands through her hair.

"Daddy was at work and Eva went to the store to get medicine. She said that Cheyenne had an ear infection and that's why she was crying all day. She said that she was coming right back, but it seemed like forever."

Michael came out of the hospital and walked to Tina. "Is that your Mom on the telephone?" Tina nodded.

"Let me speak to her." She handed him the phone. "Hey Syd. Yeah, Cheyenne is doing fine. Thanks to our big girl." He smiled at Tina. "The doctor wants to keep Cheyenne overnight for observation. Can you come and get Tina? I don't want her to have to stay cooped up here all night."

"Sure. That's no problem."

Tina tugged her dad's arm. "Daddy can I stay, too? I want to make sure Cheyenne is okay." His hesitation provoked her persistence. "Please Daddy," she hopped from foot to foot. Her hair swung in a rhythmic tempo. "I can sleep in the chair. If I can't get comfortable, then I'll call Mom to come and get me."

"I guess so." He relayed the change of plans to Sydney. "Can you come and get her if necessary?"

"I will, but our daughter is a trooper. She'll be fine."

Michael and Tina walked back into the hospital, hand in hand.

Chapter Five

Following the 11:00 A.M. Sunday service, Sydney drove from Chicago Heights to fetch Tina. She had talked to Michael earlier that morning.

"Cheyenne had a good night. The doctor released her to go home."

When Sydney got off the telephone with Michael, she called Rene and Kimberly on three-way.

"How old did you say Eva is?" Rene asked. "She should have had more sense than to leave a sick baby with a teenager."

"Eva's around twenty-five or so." Sydney flipped on the left-turn signal. "She's just a little younger than we are."

"A little younger," Rene said. "Uh, didn't you just celebrate your thirty-fifth birthday?"

"Don't even go there. You're two months and three days older than me," Sydney reminded.

"Let it go, ladies," Kimberly interjected.

"Amazing, but I agree with you Rene," Sydney said. "She should have known better. If something had happened to that baby, Michael never would have forgiven her. At least I knew how to take care of Tina. That never would have happened to me."

"Let's be fair Sydney," Kimberly added in her two cents. "You know how it is when you have your first baby. You learn by trial and error. You both are wrong. You know Eva didn't anticipate anything happening to Cheyenne."

Guilt mocked Sydney as she drove to Michael's house. "I guess I am being too hard on Eva." Ten minutes later, Sydney parked in the driveway of a two-story, newly constructed townhouse. She lifted the gold knob and rapped on the door.

"Come in," Michael said. "We're in the family room."

Sydney followed Michael through the tastefully decorated house and down two steps into the family room. Eva sat on a chair opposite the couch. She rolled her hands together and watched Tina and Cheyenne. The baby was asleep with her head resting in Tina's lap. Tina stroked her sister's face and hair.

"Hi, Mommy," Tina whispered. She put a finger on her lips and smiled down at Cheyenne. The baby stirred, opened her eyes and smiled. Tina picked up Cheyenne and cradled the baby in her arms.

"Have a seat, Sydney," Eva stood and gestured toward the chair. "I am so grateful to your daughter."

"I'm glad I insisted that Tina take the CPR class at church."

"Would you like something to drink?" Eva asked Sydney before sitting on the love seat next to her husband.

"No, I'm fine. Thank you." She turned to Tina. "Well, are you ready to go young lady? I know with all the excitement over the weekend, you didn't have a chance to do your homework."

"Oops, I forgot. I'll get my things." Michael took the baby from Tina. "Mommy can I come back next weekend and spend time with Cheyenne?"

"If it's okay with your father and Eva, I don't see why not." Sydney relaxed and sat against the back of the chair.

"She's more than welcome," Eva said.

Tina ran upstairs. She returned a few minutes later with her duffle bag. Her jacket was hanging off her right shoulder. She kissed Cheyenne and then buzzed her cheek. Cheyenne giggled and cooed. She hugged and kissed her dad and Eva. They reciprocated.

Sydney accelerated to enter the expressway. "Well, it sounds like you had a good visit with your daddy and got to know your little sister in the process." She glanced at Tina and smiled, then redirected her attention to the road.

"I did, Mommy." She dropped her head. "I didn't want to go to Daddy's house this weekend. I hated Cheyenne. I didn't want to share my daddy with her."

"It's okay baby. I knew you'd eventually come to love your sister." She patted her daughter's knee. "The Lord works in mysterious ways. You've established a relationship with your baby sister. And you and your father seem to be developing a closer bond. Now aren't you glad you went to your dad's house this weekend?"

Tina giggled. She leaned toward the dashboard and turned on the radio. "Yes, Mommy, I am."

Daddy's Girls — *A Clinical Case Study*

By Brenda McKinney, M. S., L. S. W.
Written by Valerie L. Coleman

A clinical case study of *Daddy's Girls* is provided to highlight the idiosyncrasies and innuendoes that affect relationship dynamics. The intent is to dissect actions, heighten awareness and provide techniques to avoid and resolve conflict. In this analysis, the child does not reside in the home with the stepparent; however, the tools provided apply regardless.

Chapter One

Problem: Why is Tina apprehensive about visiting her father?

Children have a natural instinct to want their biological parents together. Anyone who is perceived as an intruder may become the target of manipulation. The child thrives on making the stepparent miserable and will try to find everything wrong about the stepparent, not giving any praise or acceptance.

Symptoms:

This manipulation is a defense mechanism to overcome the fear of rejection or loss. Actions may be subtle or blatant. Subtle actions include short snappy answers, the "I don't know" response and sarcasm. Denial is another form of subtle manipulation. In this scenario, Tina's excuse about not having anything to wear and not acknowledging Cheyenne as her sister are examples of denial. It is important to note that men typically miss the subtle cues exchanged between women. The subtle manipulation is not perceived as disrespect and oftentimes goes unaddressed. The root of blatant manipulation is anger. Because children have difficulty communicating their feelings it comes out through aggressive behavior. This behavior includes fighting, threatening, self-mutilation, destruction of property, poor school progress and discord between peers and authority figures.

Depression is defined as anger turned inward. Symptoms of inward anger include change in appetite and sleep habits, isolation from others, lack of interest, boredom, anxiety and the tendency to become easily aggravated or agitated.

Cause:

Tina fears that she has lost her position as daddy's girl and therefore lost his love. From his love, stems their relationship, quality time together and a stable environment. A child will do anything in his or her power to ensure that the love is not taken away, not realizing that it never left. This sense of rejection breeds low self-esteem and self-blame that is projected onto the stepparent.

- o What's wrong with me?
- o What did I do to make them divorce?
- o I'm not good enough or pretty enough.
- o If I hadn't acted up they would have stayed together.

Although Tina is desperate for her father's love, anxiety keeps her from wanting to spend time with him. She fears the unknown.

- o Who is Eva?
- o What's she like?
- o How will we interact?

The greatest source of anxiety is probably the fear of her mother's response to the development of a relationship with Eva. Tina has an allegiance to her mother, the custodial parent, and may sabotage the relationship with Eva. Also, if a relationship is established, Tina may not divulge it to her mother or she may act indifferent toward Eva in her mother's presence. The intent is to appease her mother.

<u>Solution:</u>

The biological parents, especially the custodial parent, must give the child permission to like the stepparent by empowerment through affirmation. For example, setting the ground rules for expected behavior could include instructions such as:

- o "When you go to Eva's, respect her house as you do mine."
- o "Remember, my rules travel with you. They don't stay at the house."

Empowerment and support from the non-custodial parent is critical to the development of a healthy blended family. The child must see that all of the parents are a united front. The parents must continue to reinforce their stance as the child tries to overstep boundaries and challenge authority. Without cooperation between adults, a common vision becomes division allowing the child to divide and conquer.

The last form of empowerment develops through the exchange between the stepparent and the stepchild. Self-empowerment centers on mutual respect — I'll respect you and you'll respect me. This interaction is adapted from the "CKP" model or "Consideration, Kindness and Politeness."

- o Consideration — Be considerate of my home, my feelings, my space and privacy, my personal time with my mate/parent, my relationship with my mate/parent.
- o Kindness — speak when entering my house.

o Politeness — the manner in which the message is delivered.

While this case study deals from the perspective of the child, note that the custodial parent may also be dealing with the hurt of the lost relationship. As a result, the character and credibility of the stepparent may be in question. Developing an amicable relationship between the custodial parent and stepparent will help ease the tension and anxiety. Trust must be earned if the blended family is to survive and ultimately thrive.

Validation is another tool to build a cohesive family unit. In this scenario, Michael validated Tina's worth to him by telling her that he had waited all weekend to spend time with her. Addressing her with a term of endearment, Princess, helped to alleviate some of her concern. Just showing up as promised validated his love for her.

Empathy helps to validate the child's feelings. Acknowledging that you realize the child is apprehensive says a lot. For example, "I know the divorce is not an easy adjustment for you," lends to open communication and ease of the child's fears. When Sydney gave her permission to call home, she decreased Tina's anxiety and encouraged a sense of security.

A form of indirect validation came from Tina's mother when she reinforced that her father was looking forward to seeing her. The physical contact of touching and hugging was another form of reassurance. Caution: Stepparents must take care in touching a child that does not want to be touched. An innocent attempt to bond may be perceived as intrusive behavior and the child may become defensive.

Everyone in a blended family is looking for acceptance. Children, stepparents, custodial and non-custodial parents will confuse the need for acceptance with rejection. As a subconscious attempt at self-preservation, members retreat to the "I'll-reject-you-before-you-reject-me" mentality.

A word of caution: Parents must model the behavior they want their children to exhibit. Children watch every move and become master mimics. It is imperative that the parents, biological and step, do not speak negatively about each other, especially in the presence of the child. This action undermines the integrity of the parent and lends itself to disrespect.

Scriptural References:

Affirmation

I will praise Thee; for I am fearfully and wonderfully made (Psalm 139:14).

We are more than conquerors through Him that loved us (Romans 8:37).

I can do all things through Christ which strengthens me (Philippians 4:13).

Power of Words

Keep thy tongue from evil, and thy lips from speaking guile (Psalm 34:13).

The tongue of the wise uses knowledge aright: but the mouth of fools pour out foolishness (Proverbs 15:2).

A wholesome tongue is a tree of life: but perverseness therein is a breach in the spirit (Proverbs 15:4).

Power of life and death is in the tongue (Proverbs 18:21).

She opens her mouth with wisdom: and in her tongue is the law of kindness (Proverbs 31:26).

Chapter Two

Fair Is Fair

Adolescents are stuck on equitability, especially within the family. While visiting her father, Tina took inventory of several perceived imbalances.

Prior to the divorce, Friday night was reserved for Michael and Tina. She expected to continue their father-daughter tradition, since Eva had access to Michael all the time. Eva intruded when she sat between them on the couch. Not only did Eva become a physical wedge, she sat next to Tina, thus further overstepping her boundaries. Space invader. This action was perceived as a positional power play. Children cannot always communicate their feelings, so they use nonverbal cues. When Tina sat on the floor, she nonverbally communicated "you're in my space," without being disrespectful. Parents need to be sensitive to a child's nonverbal actions.

Eva's attempt to engage Tina in a conversation only created more anxiety. With her low self-esteem and apprehension for her stepmother, Eva's acknowledgment of being a cheerleader cut through Tina like a heated knife through butter. Cheerleading represents attractive, popular, good grades — slap after slap in Tina's face. Her body dropped to the floor, as did her emotions, like a cheerleader whose squad ran off while she was in mid-air.

Given age and maturity, it is important for children to understand that the non-custodial parent is paying support. The underlying message is that the non-custodial parent is responsible and cares about the well-being and needs of the child. It substantiates fairness, inclusion and acceptance. It shows continuity of provision for the child in spite of the new family. When Michael told Tina that he had to work overtime to pay child support, she heard, "I still love you."

Michael observed Tina's reaction to the Cheyenne shrine and immediately validated her. Explaining his time constraints and touching her back helped to alleviate some anxiety.

<u>The Green-Eyed Monster</u>

Beyond fairness, Tina is jealous of the relationship between her father and Cheyenne, as evidenced by the goose bumps. The envious monster showed up as the wicked stepmother departed. The baby had taken her place. She watched them from the corner of her eye because she did not want to see the interaction. But at the same time, she wanted to witness how she used to play with her dad.

Everyone involved in this transition goes through a period of envy, often at the same time. Assumptions are being made however no one is verbalizing his or her feelings. Unresolved misunderstandings become the foundation for dysfunctional relationships. Parents must create an atmosphere where the children feel safe to express their feelings without risk of being judged or having their feelings discounted. Children must be encouraged to experience their feelings without hearing, "You shouldn't feel like that."

Chapter Three

<u>Breaking the Ice</u>

By taking blame for the pizza, Michael mediated Tina's issue with the meat. Tina, however, did not take responsibility for her reaction. She used the incident as a means to find fault with Eva and justified her own actions. If Michael had confronted Tina's behavior at mealtime and accepted responsibility for the meaty pizza in the presence of both Tina and Eva, he may have brought a faster resolve to the problem. His response may have broken the ice and opened communication, verbal and nonverbal. They needed an out and Michael missed it. So, Tina and Eva went to bed upset and disappointed.

Michael's insistence on the shopping excursion may have forced the relationship with Tina and Eva. He needs to buffer their interaction until they feel more comfortable with one another. Tina and Eva were already apprehensive and forcing them to spend time together could further hinder healthy development of the relationship.

Defiance

As a typical teenager, Tina is full of attitude. When she flashed moose ears at Cheyenne, she transferred her aggression from her father for making her go to the mall and directed it toward her sister. Although her behavior was unacceptable, she did not blatantly disrespect her father.

Tina's uncertainty about Eva and their interaction bred anxiety and fear. She questioned whether she measured up and established expectations for herself that were not outwardly spoken. These implicit, or self-created, demands can have a major impact on the relationship, especially in a new one. Explicit expectations, or those placed upon others, have also been formed. Tina prejudged Eva's actions and assumed the mall trip would be a disaster.

The First Attempt

When Tina opted to drop the scrambled egg issue, she made a conscious decision to compromise. If a family is going to have a successful blending experience, compromise is inevitable.

Eva tried to alleviate tension by offering her undivided attention to Tina. Her communication of the day's events let Tina know what to expect. Children need structure to function effectively. Setting guidelines and expectations, scheduling specific events and activities helps them to focus and plan.

Tina displayed avoidance by rushing her meal and slipping away to her bedroom. She grabbed her personal space — the same room she disliked became her refuge. Instead of running away, she should have offered to wash the dishes or at least rinsed her dish. The number one complaint from parents is children's lack of responsibility with respect to chores, especially dishes, cleaning their bedroom and doing homework.

While on the phone with her daughter, Sydney reinforced her position that the visit was good for Tina and encouraged her to develop a relationship with her sister. Denial caused Tina to state that Cheyenne was not her sister. Her apprehension also forced her to attempt negotiations with Eva to avoid babysitting. She resisted the opportunity to help.

The Transformation

The pain of her sister brought out compassion in Tina. She took a good look at Cheyenne and liked the fact that they resembled one another. She identified with her face and developed a sense of belonging; the sisterhood was formed.

When all else failed, Tina prayed. How did she know to turn to God? Prayer may have been Tina's foundation, an essential element for the existence of families. Praying in the home sets the atmosphere for a child's healthy development. It can also be used as a coping skill and problem-solving tool. Family prayer is a good reference for survival that helps overcome stressors of every day living. Remember, "The family that prays together stays together."

Priceless

In the midst of this traumatic event, Michael took time to affirm Tina's actions to save her sister. He acknowledged her contribution and validated her position as important in the family.

Chapter Four

Acceptance

Tina acknowledged Cheyenne as her sister, not her daddy's baby and not her half-sister. This life-threatening event transformed her denial into acceptance. The pivotal moment also marked Tina's self-actualization — love for family and sense of belonging — a significant tier in Maslow's Hierarchy of Need.

When Eva said, "I don't know if I could have done what you did," she expressed appreciation, gratitude and humility. Her words indicated a sense of trust — Eva trusting Tina, and Tina trusting herself and God.

Tina accepted, yet downplayed, the compliment. She did not try to take God's glory or be boastful about saving her sister's life. She was proud of herself, but not high-minded — an admiral quality.

Life Is a Series of Choices — Choose Life or Choose Death

When Michael asked Tina if she wanted him to stay with her or go with Eva, he served a dual purpose — acknowledging her importance in the situation and letting her choose between two options. Children need choices, options and alternatives.

For example, you've decided to treat your children to lunch at a restaurant. Instead of asking them where they'd like to eat, then rejecting their options because of cost, location or quality of food, give them a choice between two or three restaurants and then honor their request. Here's another example — you want your child to wash the dishes, however, he or she is resistant. Set the boundaries and adhere to them. "You can either wash the dishes now and get it over with, or for every minute you delay, a minute will be deducted from your time on the computer." The dishes get washed with either option and the child has been empowered. This technique teaches decision making, reinforces obedience without hostility or violence and develops responsibility for the choice made.

An oppositional defiant child needs to be constrained by offering fewer options. Remember, don't get into a verbal power struggle with the child, but rather propose alternatives. Teenagers can out-talk an adult without much difficulty. Empower the child to cooperate and make a decision, instead of forcing the matter and breeding rebellion.

More Affirmation

When Sydney expressed her pride in Tina's actions, she increased her child's self-esteem tremendously. While on the phone with Sydney, Michael affirmed Tina directly when he smiled at her and indirectly when he said "Thanks to our big girl." As parents, we must stroke and encourage our children. Words of praise and affirmation are vital to the healthy development of all children, especially teenagers. Adolescents need positive encouragement to thrive just as a newborn baby needs human touch.

Young people need coaches to help them perform for peers, teachers, parents, etc. Coaches reinforce a positive behavior with a positive reward — a pat on the back. Michael coached Tina's performance and acknowledged how well she did, thus creating an environment to continue the cycle of success.

Chapter Five

Sydney allowed peer pressure to influence her actions. Rene's comment about Eva's presumed irresponsibility can be classified as gossip. Their conversation could have forged a wider chasm between the parties, if the backbiting had gotten back to Eva. What does the Word say about gossip? Has Sydney modeled gossiping before, therefore giving Rene just cause to introduce the comment into their conversation?

Parents must model the behavior they expect from their children. Leading by example versus verbal instruction speaks volumes to a child. Be mindful that parents can model both positive and negative behavior. What do your actions say to your children? Do they complement your words or contradict them?

Alliance Versus Alienation

Sydney discredited Eva as a mother by comparing her assumed response to the crisis to Eva's actions. This conversation was the opportune time to seek alliance — an essential component for all parties in a blended family. Eva already felt alienated for having left the baby with Tina. She needed alliance. The girlfriends dispatched a spirit of alienation against Eva. Kimberly, the voice of reason, rebuked both her friends for their comments. What was Sydney's motive for tearing down Eva?

Filthy communication about the biological parent confuses the child because it goes against the child's nature. Children innately show allegiance to their parents. They love unconditionally. Verbal attacks against the other parents can hinder alliance and allegiance, thus negatively affecting the relationship. Disqualifying them leads to division and ultimately, disrespect. The rules of respect are simple:

- o Do not try to get even.
- o Treat people the way you want to be treated.
- o Do not spread gossip.

The world has taught us that respect is not granted, but earned. However, that is contrary to the Word. God commands us to love and respect unconditionally regardless of our perception of a person. As His children, we must never talk negatively about the biological parent or stepparent and especially not in the child's presence.

Oneness

Sydney included Michael and Eva together when granting Tina permission to return. She did not try to single the relationship by isolating Michael as the only influential parent — an attempt to discount the position of the stepparent. She put them together as one and acknowledged Eva's entitlement as Michael's wife and a significant adult authority to Tina. Children attempt to defy the authority of the stepparent; however approval from the biological parents helps to substantiate their position. Be aware that children may misbehave because they perceive the other parent does not want them to get along with the stepparent.

Because Sydney validated Eva she released Tina to express her feelings without fear of retaliation or rejection. In essence, Tina kissed Eva with her mother's blessing.

Remember Me

By Vanessa Miller

This fictional account is loosely based on the Old Testament story of Hannah's plea for a child of her own (I Samuel 1:1– 2:36).

She tightened her grip on the receiver. *I'm going to kill him*, Hannah thought as she listened to the man on the other end ask, "Is Mr. Thomas Elk in?"

Every time she answered the phone and heard the professional tone of the person asking to speak with her husband, she learned about another past due bill. "He's not in right now. I'm his wife, can I help you?"

"Mrs. Elk, we've been trying to reach your husband concerning some very important personal business."

Hannah rubbed the spot behind her left ear where hair used to reside. Her hair had slowly fallen out as each layer of her husband's ten thousand dollars worth of personal business was revealed. "What's this about?" she asked.

"Tell your husband that if we don't receive a payment by next week, we're coming to pick up the car."

She closed her eyes as several strands of hair drifted toward the carpeted floor. She placed the phone on the receiver and grabbed the keys out of her purse. "So that's why he's been keeping his car in the garage and driving mine."

She was tired of the deception. When they first married sixteen months ago, she sat with her husband and mapped out a plan to pay every single creditor he owed. She'd even taken money out of her 401-k to make it happen within the eight-month period they'd allotted to get it done. She opened the garage door, got in her husband's silver and black Lincoln and backed it into the driveway. She turned off the ignition and got out of the car. "Come and get it." As she turned to walk into the house, Thomas pulled into the driveway with another source of deception — his son.

When they were engaged, Thomas claimed to be just as childless as she. He said that he wanted nothing more than to have a child with her, so that he could finally be a father. But seven months after the wedding ceremony, a summons for a paternity test appeared in their mailbox.

Thomas swore on a stack of Bibles, "That kid ain't mine. His mama is just trying to put him off on me so she can get some child support." She should have known he was lying. If the woman was after child support she would have picked on someone other than $27,000-a-year-earning Thomas Elk.

But even lying on a stack of Bibles couldn't change a child's DNA. Thomas was the father. "Hey baby," he said as his four year-old Mini-Me tossed a baseball to him. "Why'd you take my car out of the garage?"

Hannah turned and stared at them. How could he not know that this child was his? They had the same sandy brown complexion, same crooked smile. They even walked the same: head tilted to the side, favoring the right leg, so the sole of the shoe wore down on the right side first. *I swear to you, baby. I'm not Christopher's father.* Her husband's words rang through her ears every second and fourth Friday through Sunday. She hadn't married a doubting Thomas; hers was a liar and a deceiver. And she was sick and tired of playing his games. "While you're out playing with that baseball, the creditors are looking for your car. I'm not going to help you hide it from them." She opened the door, turned her back on her husband and his prodigal seed, and then went inside their small house.

They bought their home as soon as her husband's credit problems had been corrected. She was proud of their accomplishments and had once thought of this house as cozy. But when Christopher came to visit, she could find no place to hide. The living room and dining room were connected and the kitchen was so small she could barely flip a pancake, let alone turn around in it.

Standing in the dining room she debated her escape when Christopher walked into the house. He stood in the living room and said, "Hi, Hannah."

Hannah wouldn't even look at him. He was just trying to let her know that she hadn't said a mumbling word to him and she was not about to have her manners corrected by a four-year-old. She waved her hand in the air as she stood in the dining room. "I'm a little upset right now, Christopher. I don't feel like talking."

Thomas closed the door as he walked in. "You don't have to treat him like that Hannah. None of this is his fault."

She knew it wasn't Christopher's fault. She didn't want to mistreat him. But no matter how she tried, she couldn't force herself to do right by this little boy who had invaded her life. Instead of addressing the issue, she verbally attacked her husband. "You are the most irresponsible man I know. You know we've got all these bills, but are you out trying to get a second job?" She pointed at the baseball in his hands as though it offended her. "No, you're out playing catch." She rolled her eyes and walked out of the room.

~ ~ ~ ~ ~ ~ ~

Thomas lowered his head. Defeated. He had hoped that she would never find out about his most recent financial woes.

He'd worked three doubles in the last two weeks to come up with the extra money he needed to pay his car note. He mailed the check into them yesterday, just as he told them he would. Why did they have to call his house and upset his wife?

He handed the baseball and mitt to Christopher. "Take this stuff to your room and change out of those dirty clothes while I talk with Hannah."

"Okay." Christopher headed toward his room, then stopped and turned back around. "Hey, Dad?"

"Yes, son?"

"I had fun playing catch, but if Hannah is going to get mad we don't have to play anymore." Christopher's shoulders slumped as he turned and walked toward his room.

Thomas watched his son walk away. It tore him up to see the little guy so sad. He wanted to tell him that Hannah wasn't upset with him. But the boy was smart; he knew mistreatment when he received it. Thomas knew what it felt like also. His shoulders slumped just like his son's as he turned toward his own bedroom.

He put a smile on his face as he opened the door to his bedroom. The smile faded as he watched his wife throw her clothes into an overnight bag. "What are you doing?"

"You're a smart man, figure it out." She opened the dresser drawer, pulled out some under clothes and tossed them in her bag. "I cannot stay here one second longer. I need some time away."

His wife was the most beautiful woman he'd ever met. And although he loved her olive skin, hazel eyes and high cheek bones, it wasn't her outer layer that most attracted him. She had a big heart. She was giving and understanding. She had walked through the fire with him and helped him to become a better man. But lately, it seemed as though her inner beauty was fading. Still, he didn't want to live a day without her. "Don't leave, Hannah. If this is about my car note, I paid it yesterday." She kept packing. "Stop this honey. I can explain why it was late."

She ignored him and tried to open the bottom dresser drawer. The handle broke off in her hand. She swung around to face her husband with the object held high. "Do you see this? You promised we would get a new bedroom set, but did I get it?"

Hannah's mother had given them their bedroom set and the cream colored leather sofa and chair in their living room as well. But the bedroom set was more than a decade old when she'd passed it down to them. The wood had faded in spots and bubbled in others. He wanted desperately to buy his queen something she could be proud of — he wanted to be someone she could be proud of. He hadn't brought much of anything to this marriage. Well that wasn't true — he'd brought ten thousand in debt and a four-year-old son. Neither of which Hannah appreciated. "I'm working on it. If you give me some time, I'll make good on all my promises to you."

She harrumphed as she put the last of her items in the overnight bag and zipped it. "Time is running out on your caviar dreams and champagne wishes."

He lowered his voice to a whisper. "I didn't expect to be paying child support. I'm trying to get adjusted to having three hundred dollars a month taken out of my paycheck. You helped me with all the debt I had when we first got married, why can't you work with me on this?"

Rolling her eyes for the second time that day, she picked up her bag, opened the bedroom door and walked past him. "I'll be at my sister's for the weekend. We'll talk when I get back."

~ ~ ~ ~ ~ ~ ~ ~

Hannah sat in her sister's expansive kitchen, dipping her fresh-out-of-the-oven oatmeal cookie into ice cold milk. Her favorite remedy to the blues. Her big sister knew her so well. "Janice you just don't know what it's like. I can't take it anymore. Thomas was not truthful with me and I shouldn't have to stay married to a man like that."

Janice put another batch of oatmeal cookies in the oven, then sat behind the island and put her elbows on the marble counter top. "What makes you think I don't know how it is?"

Hannah put another warm, ooey-gooey cookie in her mouth and waved her arm in dramatic fashion. "Look at all you have. This huge house with non-hand-me-down furniture is evidence enough that your husband treats you good. This place has to be at least 4,000 square feet."

Janice laughed. "4,500 to be exact. But little sis, I think you're forgetting something."

"You're doggone right I forgot something." She stepped down from the high-back stool and walked to the great room. The name was no exaggeration. From the cathedral ceiling to the Pella windows and the open fireplace, not to mention the snow-white carpet and lounging furniture — spectacular. "I forgot how to live good, is what I forgot." She turned to face her sister as she heard footsteps behind her. "I feel like I live in a shoe when I come over here. Everything is so big and roomy, while I can barely turn around without knocking something over in my house."

Janice put her sister's hand in hers. "It didn't start off like this, Hannah." She squeezed her hands. "Don't you remember that little apartment John and I had on Wabash?" Janice laughed as she released her sister's hand. "Girl, some days I thought the roaches were eating more food than we were."

"I remember that apartment."

"Come sit with me," Janice told Hannah. They walked out of the snow-white room and entered the family room. The place for all things beige and comfortable. They sat together on the sectional. "It took a lot of years before John and I were able to live comfortable. We struggled for the first nine years of our marriage."

Hannah knew all about struggling. She was majoring in it — at the school of hard knocks. "Didn't you get tired?"

"Of course I did. Those were the nights when I did a lot of crying and a lot of praying. I still can't explain how it all worked out; I just know that God answers prayers. And I think He has a special place in His heart for a crying woman."

A tear trickled down Hannah's cheek. "But John didn't have to pay child support or spend time with a child that didn't belong to the both of you."

Janice wiped the tear from her sister's face. "No he didn't, but he had other problems and so did I. But we worked together to solve them. I'm telling you what I know, Hannah. With God's help you can get through this."

Head bowed low, Hannah confessed, "I haven't prayed much lately."

Janice scooted closer to her sister and put her arm around her. "God's still on the throne, sweetie. He hasn't changed residence — you can still find Him if you seek after Him."

She and her sister talked well into the night. Then Janice told her that she needed to go make her man happy. Hannah went to the guest room and climbed in bed, but she couldn't get to sleep. She was too busy wondering why she couldn't get past the anger and work with Thomas. If her sister could work with her husband and move her family from poverty to prosperity, why couldn't she do the same? Why was she so angry all the time? Her husband was good to her and she loved him.

About three in the morning, she admitted to herself where the greatest part of her anger stemmed. She hadn't conceived. She and Thomas had been trying to have a baby for over a year — and nothing. She didn't have many childbearing years left. If something didn't happen soon... Every time she saw Christopher, it was like a reminder of her failure to conceive a child for the man she loved. Consequently, even surrounded by her husband's love, she was miserable.

She told Thomas how she felt a couple months back and he asked her, "Isn't my love enough for you, Hannah?" She pulled the covers tight around her barren body. She hadn't been able to answer his question then and she still didn't know if his love was enough to quiet the turmoil in her soul.

~ ~ ~ ~ ~ ~ ~

On Sunday morning, Thomas got up early to make Christopher's favorite breakfast: cinnamon pancakes with chocolate milk. Thomas learned more and more about his son each weekend they spent together. He enjoyed getting to know his son. The only unfortunate part of the time he spent with his child was his wife's reaction. But he had denied and neglected Christopher for too long, no way he would continue to be a dead-beat dad. Yeah, he was paying child support, but sending money didn't make you a dad. Families invested time in one another. If he only got one thing right in his life — he wanted to be a great father. He wanted Christopher to grow up and tell his son that he had a father who did everything he could and even went that extra mile to ensure that he led a successful life.

The telephone rang as Thomas sprinkled powered sugar on Christopher's pancakes. He hoped it was his wife calling to say she was on her way home. But a glance at the caller ID told him it was his best friend, Sam Johnson. Thomas smiled. His first since Hannah walked out on Friday. Sam was his boy. He had the ability to make him believe that everything would be all right. They'd been boys for a long time. They went to the same elementary, same high school. Played on the same basketball team, went on double dates together. Married months apart from each other. They'd done everything together. Well, everything, but....

"You still coming to church with me today?" Sam asked.

Sam had given his life to Jesus without Thomas' consent or approval. These days Thomas' opinion didn't seem to carry much weight with Sam. It was all about how the Lord expected him to live and what he discovered in prayer. And now his boy was getting baptized. "Man, I totally forgot."

Sadness crept into Sam's voice. "Don't tell me that you won't be there. This is a really big event in my life."

Thomas wasn't a total heathen. He'd grown up in church and knew the importance of baptism. "I didn't say I wasn't coming. I just said I forgot. We'll get dressed and meet you there in an hour."

~ ~ ~ ~ ~ ~ ~

Hannah went to The Church On The Rock with Janice and her family. The praise and worship was electrifying. She couldn't remember when she had last lifted her hands in adoration to her King. But as the praise leader ushered the congregation into the presence of the Lord, Hannah lifted her hands and worshipped God. After praise and worship, seven congregants were baptized. Thomas' friend, Sam, was among them. Seeing Sam made her long for her husband. She lost a bit of her praise as sadness snuck in.

But when Pastor Frankson stood behind the podium, it was as if he made it his personal business to preach her happy. She wondered why she and Thomas didn't attend church more often. When they were first married they discussed how they wanted to raise their family in church. Maybe the fact that she hadn't been able to provide Thomas with a child had halted all thoughts of attending church. As if seeing into the depths of her wounded heart, Pastor Frankson talked about how his children were the joy of his life. Tears rolled down Hannah's face as she sat in her seat. She wanted to have a child. Someone to call her own. But maybe she had waited too long for marriage. She was thirty-seven and her eggs had dried up.

When Pastor Frankson finished his message, he made an altar call. Hannah remembered her sister saying that God had a special place in His heart for crying women. She stood and walked toward the altar. She didn't allow the altar workers to pray for her — she needed a direct line to God. Hannah bowed at the altar and with tears streaming down her face, admitted to God that she was mad at her husband and mad at his son because she had been denied the opportunity to be a mother.

Her lips moved, but no sound escaped as she continued to sob and pray — pray and sob. "Lord," her silent lips proclaimed, "I feel so empty without a child of my own. My husband loves me, I know that, but I need to be able to give him a child. Please help me." She told the Lord how sorry she was for neglecting to spend time with Him. "I've missed You, Lord. I won't forget about You again. I promise."

~ ~ ~ ~ ~ ~ ~

Thomas and Christopher arrived at The Church On The Rock twenty minutes late. The place was so packed he doubted they would find a seat. A kind greeter hugged them and then directed them to a seat in the back.

He missed praise and worship, but arrived just in time to give his offering to the Lord. He was so glad he hadn't missed offering. From a child, his parents taught him about bringing his first fruits into the house of the Lord. He'd always been diligent about doing just that. But the last two years had thrown him for a loop. He'd gotten off track with attending church. He hadn't been a regular since he left his parents' home, but he attended at least once a month to give his tithes. Lately though, he'd gotten off track with that too. He calculated his week's earnings and put ten percent into the collection plate.

When the pastor stood to preach, Thomas spotted Hannah in the second row. Try as he might, he couldn't keep his mind focused on the message, his eyes slipped in the direction of his wife. When the altar call was made and Hannah stood looking lost, bewildered and tormented, Thomas couldn't help but wonder if he was the cause of her pain. "Lord," he said with his head bowed, "I won't ever neglect to pay my tithes again, if You could just bring a bit of happiness into Hannah's life."

He lifted his head just as his wife knelt at the altar. He wanted to go to her, but from the distance she looked like a mad woman, a drunk even. As she cried and rocked, her mouth moved so fast, he doubted if any audible sound escaped at all. How could he go to her if he was the reason she was at the altar displaying herself in such a manner? Maybe it was time for him to let her go. He leaned over and told Christopher, "Gather your things. We need to go."

The child sat on the floor playing with his X-Men figures. He looked up. "But nobody else is leaving."

Thomas picked the X-Men off the floor and stood. "Let's go."

~ ~ ~ ~ ~ ~ ~

Driving home, Hannah felt renewed. She couldn't explain why she felt different, except that she knew God had heard her prayer. She had an audience with the King. She had received quite a few funny glances as she removed herself from the altar. She even heard a little boy ask his mother if she was drunk. But she didn't care. Her time with God had been just what she needed. She was now headed home to work on her marriage.

She debated calling Thomas to tell him she was on her way. But she had treated him so bad and had such evil thoughts of him the day she left, she was afraid of his response. She thought their reunion would go better if they were face to face. If he could see how sorry she was, then maybe he would forgive her. As she pulled into their driveway she saw Thomas and Christopher in the backyard tossing that baseball again. Irritation crawled in. She tried to shake it off as she closed her eyes and prayed, "Lord, please don't forget me. If You give me a child, I promise I will give him back to You. I will raise him to love and serve You."

What about the other child, Hannah? Who will give him back to Me?

Hannah's mouth fell slack as she pressed her hand against her chest. "My Lord, are You speaking to me?"

I want Christopher to serve Me also.

Tears rolled down her face. Was she really that selfish? Had she only thought of her own feelings and neglected what Christopher needed? What she'd discovered today was that not only did she and Thomas need God in their lives, but Christopher needed God too. At his young age, the only way Christopher would come to know God would be through the adults in his life. "Lord, forgive me. Help me to show that little boy Your love."

As she got out of the car, the bitterness surrounding the three hundred a month Thomas sent to Christopher's mother slipped from her heart. With each step she took toward her husband and his child she saw more of what Christopher needed from her and less of what she thought he was taking. As she rounded the corner, she wiped at the tears on her face and tried to smile.

Christopher had the baseball in his hand. He was getting ready to toss it to Thomas when he spotted her. He lowered the ball and then hid it behind his back. Hannah walked over to him and knelt in front of her adorable stepson. She held out her hand and asked, "Can I throw the ball to you, honey?"

Christopher's eyes widened. "You want to play with me?"

Hannah wiped more tears from her face. "Yes, I want to play with you. Is that all right?"

Christopher wrapped his small arms around her neck and squeezed. "Don't cry Hannah, I'll toss the ball to you."

Thomas joined his wife and son and draped his arms around both of them. "Thank You, Lord, for giving me back my family."

Hannah lifted her head and looked at them. That was it, wasn't it? You might be able to pick your friends, but family was a whole other matter. You take what comes and you deal with it. All the while, your heart keeps growing to accept each knew entry. Family. She would thank God for the rest of her life for the one He had blessed her with.

As the Sands of the Sea

By Valerie L. Coleman

The Bible is full of stories that deal with blended families. Jacob's wives, Leah and Rachel, were sisters that mothered nations of Israel. Solomon had hundreds of wives and concubines that produced many children.

Abraham and Sarah, consumed with forcing God's promise, created their blended family through Hagar (Genesis 16). This fictional story is loosely based on their intense living arrangements and the drama they may have encountered.

Reflections from the artificial lights bounced off the surgical equipment and made five-point stars on the ceiling. The deafening silence shot through Sammi Reid as she prepped the delivery room. "Okay, Lord. I need Your help again."

The nurses wheeled the screaming mother-to-be into the room and hooked her to the monitor. "Aaaagh! It's coming! The baby's coming!"

"Miss Lewis, I need you to take a deep breath and relax." Sammi stroked her patient's hand. "Do you remember your Lamaze exercises? Hee-hee-hee-hoo."

"Hee-hee nothing. That mess is not helping." She grabbed Sammi's smock and pulled her close. "How'd you get through this?"

Sammi forced the woman's hands from her smock and stepped back. "I don't have any children. I nev—"

"Then what good are you?" Miss Lewis fell back onto the bed and wailed in agony.

Sammi ran out of the delivery room. Tears raced down her cheeks as she darted into the restroom. By the time the assisting nurse found her, she was shriveled in the corner sobbing without restraint.

"Are you okay Nurse Reid?"

"I'll be fine." She shooed her assistant away. "Please, leave me alone Deena."

"You know women say some terrible things when they're in labor. You shouldn't take it personal."

"I can't take it any other way, but personal." She unraveled a pile of toilet paper to blow her nose. "Didn't I ask you to leave? Who's attending to Miss Lewis?"

"I've already taken care of that." Deena knelt on the floor next to Sammi and rubbed her arm. "I know how you feel."

"How can you possibly know how I feel? I've seen the pictures of your kids plastered at your work station."

"What you've seen is the end result of negative EPT readings, miscarriages and thousands of dollars in fertility treatments. My husband and I tried for fifteen years before we finally got pregnant."

Sammi perked. "Really?" She supported herself on the toilet seat and stood.

"Yeah. Before I had my babies, I spent a lot of nights asking God what I did to make Him shut my womb."

"I still do." Sammi blew her nose, then tossed the paper in the toilet and flushed. "So what finally worked for you?" The ladies washed their hands and proceeded to the staff lounge.

"Dr. Sturdivant." Deena grabbed her lunch from the refrigerator. "You should go see him. I'm living proof he's a miracle worker."

~ ~ ~ ~ ~ ~ ~

"Good morning, sweetheart." Anthony, Sammi's loving husband, greeted her with a wet peck on the lips.

"What's good about it?" Sammi slammed the glass on the table. Orange juice showered the plate of hot cakes and bacon.

"Whoa!" Anthony jumped back from the table. "What's got you going first thing in the morning?"

"Nothing." She snatched a Brawny to clean up the big mess. He took the juice-soaked towel out of her hand, caressed her chin and raised her head to meet his gaze. *Oh boy. Here we go again.* Sammi tensed.

"Nothing, huh?" He stroked her arms and pulled her toward him. Rocking his wife in his massive arms, he hummed *There's No God Like Jehovah.*

"Babe, please don't do that." She tried to pull away from his gentle, but firm, embrace. "I'm not in the mood." When he ignored her request, she added some bass to her soft soprano voice. "Tee," she attempted to break free. "I said I'm not in the mood."

"I'm not intimidated by your aggression." He squeezed a little tighter. "Just relax and wait on the Lord to sooth your spirit."

The Issey Miyake cologne combined with his natural scent calmed her. She closed her eyes and let her body go limp. In complete surrender, she buried her head in his oh-so-sexy chest and bawled. He continued to hum her favorite song. A few minutes into her monthly melt down, she regained her composure.

"Thanks, Babe." He wiped her face with a paper towel. She took it and blew her nose. "You'd think I'd be over this by now." She tossed the makeshift hanky in the trashcan and walked into the master suite to get ready for work.

~ ~ ~ ~ ~ ~ ~

"I learned about a new doctor." Sammi sopped up the runny yolk with a slice of wheat toast. "And it got me thinking."

Anthony peeked over the newspaper and then laid it on the table. "I know we've been to a lot of specialists, but he's —"

"Sammi, I know where you're headed with this. Let's just accept our lot." He scooted his chair next to hers. "I mean look at our life." He spanned his arms left and right. "We live well. God has blessed us with a beautiful home, great careers and an awesome church family." He knelt beside his wife and cupped her hands in his. "And each other. Isn't that enough?"

"No, it's not." She stood and paced the floor. "I want to know what it feels like to have life growing inside me. I want to hear a tiny heart beat. I want to look at an ultrasound and try to figure out whether we're having a boy or girl. I want to teach our children all that I have learned and show them all that the world has to offer. I want — no, I need to be made whole. And all the money in the world can't buy me that." She grabbed Anthony's ears and pulled him toward her. "Besides, you're the one who keeps having that dream."

"I know, but —"

"But nothing. What else could it mean? You're walking on the beach with a figure of light that tells you your children will be as the sands of the sea." She scooped up imaginary sand and held out her hand to allow the grains to pass through her fingers. "If that doesn't read 'baby on board,' I don't know what does."

"And you think this doctor has the answer?" He followed Sammi into the family room.

"It's worth a try. We have not because we ask not."

~ ~ ~ ~ ~ ~ ~

The doctor's waiting room housed a wall of pictures and thank-you notes from once childless parents. Grinning like the Cheshire cat from *Alice in Wonderland*, they cradled their newborns. One couple delivered triplets and named them after the nurses in the office.

"See, babe. I know he can help us."

They sat in the plush sage and ivory striped chairs. Propped on the edge of her seat, Sammi watched a lady bounce her toddler on her lap. Anthony flipped through the magazines and expelled an occasional sigh.

"Mr. and Mrs. Reid," the nurse called. "The doctor will see you now."

Sammi tailed close behind the nurse. Anthony lagged several feet back. "Oops. I'm sorry." Sammi flung her hand to her mouth. "I didn't mean to step on your shoe."

"It's okay," the nurse said, as she steadied herself on the mahogany desk. "You'd be surprised how many times a day I have to fix my shoe. A hazard of the job."

Sammi chuckled. Anthony yawned, pulled out the leather chair for his wife and then took a seat next to her. The nurse turned over the hourglass on the end table and then left the room.

"That just confirmed it," Sammi said as watched the sand trickle.

"What?"

"This," she pointed to the hourglass. "Sand, just like in your dream."

"Uh, honey, you think maybe that's how the doctor keeps time for his consultations? I doubt this has anything to do with my dream." He chuckled and leaned back in his seat.

"If you didn't want to be here, why did you come?" Sammi flopped back in her seat and slapped her arms across her chest.

"I want to support you in this, I really do. I just don't want to see you hurt again."

"Well, you've got a strange way of showing it."

He rubbed her back. "With every failed hope, you fall into a deeper rut. Then I get frustrated because I don't know what to do to help you."

Dr. Sturdivant entered the room. "Good morning." He greeted his patients with a firm handshake and walked behind the desk. "I've got the results of your tests." He sat in the studded swivel chair and rapped his fingers along the armrests.

"Yes," Sammi said. "When can we get started?"

"Well, Mrs. Reid." His tone changed from the cheerful salutation. "I regret to inform you that you will never be able to conceive a child."

Sammi's smile faded as tears formed in her brown eyes. Anthony reached for her right hand and then caressed her arm.

"What do you mean? Why can't I conceive a child? You've helped so many other people." Tears gushed like Old Faithful and fell to her lap. "You're my last hope."

"I am sorry, but your ovaries and uterus are severely scarred from the endometriosis and subsequent laparoscopies. Even if you could conceive," he shuffled through her medical records. "You would not be able to carry the fetus to term."

With her world shattered yet again, Sammi dropped her head and sobbed. Crushed, like the prey of a boa constrictor. Dr. Sturdivant handed her a box of Kleenex.

"Don't give up on me quite yet, Mrs. Reid." He reached for a brochure and handed it to her. "Have you considered surrogate parenting?"

Anthony took the brochure and skimmed through it. "You want me to have sex with another woman so Sammi and I can have a child?" He slammed the brochure on the desk. "I don't think so."

"No, Mr. Reid. Modern science has afforded us the ability to fertilize the egg in the lab and insert it in the surrogate mother. We'll use your sperm of course."

"Well how does that help me?" Sammi questioned with her head still bowed.

"Mrs. Reid, I understand that you want to experience the birth of your own biological child. However, this procedure is your best option." He walked from behind his desk and propped himself on its edge. Leaning toward Sammi, he continued, "You can select a woman with similar physical characteristics. You'll have the opportunity to review her stat sheet that includes her family medical history, educational background, likes and dislikes and a host of other things. She'll provide the egg, carry and deliver your child and then you can nurture and love it." He patted her shoulder. "You can even choose the sex of the child. All the benefits and none of the pain."

"Not all of the benefits," Sammi said. "We'll have to talk it over."

~ ~ ~ ~ ~ ~ ~

Helen was in her second trimester, when she visited. Her dark brown, shoulder-length hair danced in the refreshing spring breeze. The additional fifteen pounds added to her petite five-foot-two frame caused her ankles to swell. She waddled up to the solid oak door and pressed the intercom.

"Who is it?" Sammi said.

"Hi, Mrs. Reid. It's me, Helen."

"Oh, hi Helen. I'll be right down." She closed her laptop, ran down the stairs and flung open the door. "I wasn't expecting you today. Come on in."

"I'm sorry to come over unannounced, but I had no where else to go." She stepped into the grand foyer and waited for Sammi to close the door. "I was evicted today."

"Oh my. I'm sorry to hear that." She escorted Helen to the front sitting room. "Would you like something to drink?"

"Yes, please. A glass of water would be fine."

"Rosa, please bring us some water." She sat on the plush couch. "Tell me what happened."

"Well, my financial aid package was rejected." She rummaged in the pockets of her red windbreaker, jingling loose change. "I had hoped to get a job on campus, but no one wants the risk of hiring a roly-poly student."

"I had no idea. What can I do to help?" Rosa placed two coasters on the marble table and set a glass of iced-cold water on each one. "Thank you, Rosa."

"I know it's a lot to ask," Helen sipped the water and dropped her head. "But do you think I can stay here for a couple of days? Just until I can work something out."

"I don't see why not, but let me run it past Anthony first."

~ ~ ~ ~ ~ ~ ~

Sammi stared out the window. She watched the chilled morning air dance in the sunlight as the neighborhood kids waited for the school bus. She doodled in the condensation on the glass, until the yellow limousine drove out of sight. She walked to the oak crib and cranked the mobile. A medley of nursery rhymes played as a parade of yellow, green and white teddy bears bounced up and down.

"I knew I'd find you here." Anthony walked into the room. "You are so predictable."

"Good morning, Handsome." She hugged her man. "I can't believe we're about to have a baby."

"Well, you better start believing. He'll be here in a few weeks." He kissed her forehead. "I can't tell you're not a believer. The major dent in my wallet says otherwise."

"How do you like Ivan?" She looked up at Anthony with life in her eyes. "I think that'd be a nice name. Ivan Anthony Reid."

"It's got a nice ring to it. Especially the middle name."

Rosa entered the room. "Excuse me. Mr. Reid, Helen needs you downstairs."

"Thanks." He released his wife. "Tell her I'll be right there." He left the nursery and ran down the hall to the master suite.

What's that about? Sammi peeked out the room. Anthony hummed, as he splashed on cologne and checked his hair in the mirror. He bolted down the stairs.

Sammi wrung her hands together and tiptoed to the stairs. She sat on the top step and propped her elbows on her knees. The mumbled conversation forced her to scoot down to the landing. Lying on her stomach, she stretched to look around the corner.

Anthony and Helen gazed into each other's eyes and held hands. He gave her an envelope and said, "This will be our little secret."

They walked to the door laughing. He watched her through the etched glass in the sidelight and waved goodbye. A sinister smile creased his lips, as he turned toward the staircase. Sammi ran up the stairs and tripped on her chenille bathrobe.

"Sammi! Are you okay?" He yelled from the first floor.

"I'm fine. Just bumped into the armoire."

"That's the third time this week." He grabbed his car keys from the kitchen island. "Maybe we should rearrange the furniture."

"I've got some rearranging to do," she said under her breath. "But it ain't furniture."

~ ~ ~ ~ ~ ~ ~ ~

After an intense day at the hospital, exhaustion settled on Sammi. "I can't believe he didn't call me today." She slammed on the brakes in time to avoid a rear-end collision. "No poetic email. No love note. No 'I miss you, baby' phone call." She evil-eyed the old lady creeping along in the brown jalopy.

She tuned the satellite radio to WFCJ 93.7 FM for inspiration. She loved *Adventures in Odyssey*. In less than fifteen minutes, those characters resolved some complex problems.

"Okay, Lord." She closed her eyes to pray and then remembered she was driving. "I'm having trouble dealing with this surrogate mother thing. They are spending way too much time googling at each together." She swerved around the trashcan, as she pulled into the driveway. "Anthony insists that his recurring dream is a promise from You. He truly believes that we are supposed to raise a child together. So, Lord, if this is Your will, please help me."

She parked the Mercedes in the three-car garage and walked into the mudroom. As she hung her jacket in the closet, she heard Helen and Anthony whispering. "What are you two talking about?" Sammi drug her bags into the kitchen.

"Oh, hi honey." He sat back in his chair. "I didn't hear you come in."

Obviously. "Hi, Helen. What were you two talking about?"

"Nothing," she shoveled a fork full of medium-rare prime rib in her mouth.

"Oh, so you decided to eat without me, huh?" She bit her tongue to stifle the words fighting to come out.

"I'm sorry," he stood to help Sammi with her briefcase and purse. "I thought today was hair day. I didn't expect you until later."

"No, that's next week."

"How was your d—"

"The baby's kicking!" Helen squealed. Anthony spun around. "Feel!" Helen grabbed his hand and placed it on her tight stomach. Nine months pregnant and she was gorgeous. Her hair was fuller and halfway down her back. Her tiny nose never swelled and her breasts filled out her tops in harmony with her new hips.

"Oooo, Sammi," he reached for her hand. "Feel Ivan's elbow."

"My hands are full. I'll feel it the next time."

"Ivan? When did we decide on Ivan?" Helen furrowed her brows and smooched out her lips.

"It's not final," Anthony said. "Just a name Sammi threw out this morning." He turned back to his wife. "Are you ready to eat?"

"I'm not hungry."

~ ~ ~ ~ ~ ~ ~

The flannel grandma pajamas stuck to her body as sweat became an adhesive. Two seconds after the door to Helen's room closed, Anthony walked into the bedroom.

"Babe, are you asleep?" He leaned over Sammi and whispered, "Babe?" He walked to his side of the king-size poster bed, set the alarm clock and then went into the adjoining bathroom. A few minutes later, he climbed into bed and snuggled behind his wife.

Sammi snatched the covers and tucked them under her side. "It's time for Helen to go."

~ ~ ~ ~ ~ ~ ~

Ahh. The scent of a newborn is so sweet. Pure. Untouched. Innocent. Natural. Anthony sniffed his son's neck and smiled. He counted each little finger and toe. He took in one big breath and handed the baby to Sammi.

"He's so handsome," she said, as a lone tear rolled down her cheek. "He really favors you Anthony." The baby cooed and nestled her bosom. "Uh-oh, I think he's hungry." She gave Helen the baby. "How long will you be breast-feeding him?"

"The doctor said that the first few days are most important." She propped him in her arms and pulled the gown off her shoulder. "It helps build up his immunities."

Sammi grabbed the receiving blanket and placed it over Helen's right breast. "We've got to be discreet. There's a man in the room."

"Oh, I'm sorry." She adjusted the blanket. "Everyone on this floor has seen my goodies. If I ever had any shame, it's long gone now."

~ ~ ~ ~ ~ ~ ~

Three days later, Sammi and Anthony arrived at the hospital to take Ivan home. Helen cradled him in her arms, as they entered the room.

"I didn't think this would be so hard," she said, as she caressed her baby's face. A tear rolled down her cheek. "I think I made a mistake."

"Nonsense," Sammi said, with her arms out stretched. "You've been used by God to fulfill His promise to us. How can that be a mistake?" She took Ivan. "You can come by and visit him whenever you like — as long as you call ahead first."

"Thanks again, Helen," Anthony said with his hand on her shoulder. "Would you like a few minutes alone with him before we leave?"

"Uh-hum," Sammi cleared her throat and threw a what-are-you-thinking look at her husband. "We really need to get him home, honey. We've got family and friends coming over this afternoon."

"She's right. You better leave." Helen dropped her head and slouched under the covers. As Sammi and Anthony walked out of the hospital room, she wept.

~ ~ ~ ~ ~ ~ ~

"Oh, Sammi, he is soooo cute," Deena, her co-worker, said while oochie-coochie-cooing the baby in her lap.

"He looks a lot like Anthony when he was a baby," Sammi's mother-in-law said. "I guess the dimples come from his mother, huh?"

"I am his mother."

Anthony interjected. "Mom, I thought you said that Daddy's great grandfather had dimples."

"Oh yeah, I forgot about that. Sorry."

Trying to change the subject, Deena asked, "So Sammi, how long will you be off work?"

"I took a one-year leave of absence. Depending upon how things go after that, I may just quit and be a stay-home mom."

"That is so nice. I'm really happy for you," Deena said.

"Here, Beautiful." Anthony handed Sammi a gift wrapped in teddy bear paper.

"What's this?"

"Just open it." With great care, she removed the ribbon and each piece of tape. "Good grief. I've got more paper. Rip into it woman."

"Excuse me, but I will be keeping every last piece of paper, ribbon and any other memento of my baby." She folded the paper and then opened the box. "Oh, Anthony. It's beautiful!" She lifted the box to show her guests a customized baby book.

Raised letters spelled out Ivan's full name and birth date. Embellished with seashells, the cover had a picture of Sammi kissing her newborn. The inscription on the first page read, "As the sands of the sea…"

Tears welled in her eyes as she flipped through the pages. The family tree traced back their genealogy five generations. Ivan's development, displayed in framed ultra sound photos, had cute captions like "Daddy's favorite" and "Ready or not, here I come."

"How did you put all this together?"

"I didn't. Helen did it."

"Helen?" Sammi swallowed hard and looked at her husband. A question mark dangled over her head.

"Yeah. She loves to make scrapbooks and asked me if I thought you'd want one. She really poured her heart into it." He took the book and perused the craftsmanship. "I've been giving her stuff for quite some time."

"In envelopes?"

~ ~ ~ ~ ~ ~ ~

The door bell chimed a medley of tunes.

"Hola, Señorita Helen."

"Hola, Rosa."

"Please come in and take a seat. I will get Mrs. Reid."

"Thank you." Helen sat on the chaise lounge and spanned the room. The custom-framed artwork carried a family theme. Shades of green, burgundy and ivory created an atmosphere of warmth and tranquility. She stood and then walked to the lighted curio. It displayed angel figurines and pictures of the Reid family. "That should be my family."

"Hi, Helen," Sammi said as she entered the room. She closed the French doors behind her.

"Oh, hi." She stepped back from the curio and took a seat.

"I didn't know you were coming by today. Did I miss your message?" Sammi stood next to the curio and wiped the smudges off the glass.

"No, no message. I was just in the neighborhood, so I decided to stop by and visit with Ivan."

"I really wish you had called first." She walked to Helen and stood over her. "He's asleep right now."

"Can't you wake him? I haven't seen him in a couple of months."

"Sorry. He's been a little temperamental lately. He's teething." She looked down at Helen. "No one prevented you from coming, so where have you been?"

"My financial aid package finally came in, so I'm back at school. And I've gotten a job on campus. By the time I get done, it's too late to visit."

Well, if you really wanted to see him, you'd make time. "I understand." She opened the French doors.

"I got your thank-you card. That was really nice." Helen stood.

"You're welcome. I just wanted to let you know how much I appreciated the scrapbook." Sammi walked toward the front door.

"I didn't understand your comment though."

"What comment was that?"

"All is forgiven." She rummaged through her purse for the car keys. "What did that mean?"

"Did I put that in your card? I meant to write 'All is for Ivan.' Guess I had too much on my mind." She opened the front door.

"Oh, okay." Helen stepped onto the porch and then turned around. "Do you think I can get Ivan for the weekend?"

"I'm not too sure about that."

"I just want to spend some time with him."

"Yeah, well —"

"Well what? He is my son," Helen threw her hands on her tiny hips and shifted her neck side-to-side.

"Correction. He's my son."

~ ~ ~ ~ ~ ~ ~

At ten months old, Ivan propped himself on the family room table, then stood unsupported.

"Oh my goodness," Sammi said. "He's standing!" At that moment, Ivan teetered and began to fall. Sammi ran to catch him.

"Whew, that was close," Anthony said as he ran into the room.

"Yeah, I almost didn't get to him in time," she said panting. "I don't know what's going on with me, but I've been so tired lately." She hugged Ivan and then sat on the couch.

"You have been sleeping a lot." Anthony reached over, tickled his son and then kissed his wife. "You're probably tired from running after him all day."

"I guess. I never imagined motherhood could be so rewarding and tiring at the same time."

That evening, Anthony was awakened by the sound of Ralph and Earl being introduced to the porcelain king. "Babe, are you okay?"

"I think I ate too much at dinner." She moaned and then continued the introductions. Anthony wet a washcloth and held it on her forehead. "Thanks, Handsome."

"I think you should see a doctor. Weight loss and tiredness are symptoms of diabetes and you know that runs in your family."

Four weeks later, she had an appointment at Horizon Women's Healthcare with Dr. Andre Harris. "Well, Mrs. Reid, you'll be glad to know that you do not have diabetes."

"Then what's wrong with me Dr. Dre?"

"Nothing's wrong. You're pregnant."

~ ~ ~ ~ ~ ~ ~ ~

Still in disbelief from the doctor's news, Sammi laughed all the way home. Her hysteria escalated at each traffic light. By the time she got home, she had wet her pants. "He must think I'm stupid. I'm forty-five years old. My missed period is menopause, not pregnancy." She slipped out of her clothes and jumped in the shower. "I'm not even going to bother Tee with this one. He's had enough disappointment."

After getting dressed, Sammi met her husband for lunch at an outdoor bistro. "So what'd the doctor say? Are you diabetic?"

"Nope," she sipped on the raspberry lemonade.

"Whew, what a relief. So what did he say about your symptoms?"

"He's clueless," she stared at the straw in her iced drink.

"Clueless? That doesn't sound like Dr. Dre."

"Well, he didn't have a reasonable explanation," she opened the menu. "I think I'll have the bruschetta chicken."

~ ~ ~ ~ ~ ~ ~ ~

Mountains of fresh produce towered over the customers in pursuit of a temporary price reduction. Sammi grabbed a couple of white grapes and popped them in her mouth.

"Now is that becoming of a saint?" Anthony said.

"You weren't supposed to see that."

"Well I did." He placed some oranges in the cart.

Ivan reached for the sun-kissed goodies. "Eat-eat."

"See what you started."

213

"Forgive me, Lord." She said with a huff. "Happy now?"

He chuckled. "What else do we need for the party?"

"Well, I'm expecting about seventy people. Do we have enough charcoal and lighter fluid to grill all the meat?"

"Not sure. I'll get some and then meet you at the register."

Sammi tossed a couple more grapes in her mouth and handed one to Ivan. She searched for the perfect strawberries for his birthday cake.

"Hi, little man," Helen said as she tickled Ivan's side. He whimpered.

Sammi spun around. "Excuse me. Why are you poking my son?"

"I didn't poke him. I tickled him."

"Then why is he crying?" Sammi unfastened his seat belt and lifted him out of the cart. "It's okay, momma's baby." She patted his back and bounced him, as she sneered at Helen. She propped him on her right hip and continued to sort through the strawberries.

"I didn't mean to make him cry. Sorry." She moved next to Sammi and pretended to have an interest in the fruit. "Got anything special planned for his birthday?"

"Not really. Just having a simple get together. Nothing spectacular."

"Mind if I drop by then?"

"No, that's not going to work."

"I don't understand why you're being so evasive. I just want to spend time with my son. I-I mean, with Ivan."

Sammi rolled her eyes. "To be totally honest, I'm not comfortable with you being around my son."

"But why? I've never done anything to him."

"Look, I really don't have time right now and I do not have to explain myself to you. It's better for Ivan if you don't keep popping in and out of his life." She shifted him to her other hip. "We've been more than obliging, allowing you to have as much time with him as you have."

"Allowing me? I'm his mother. I have rights too."

"Sorry sweetie. When you signed on the dotted line and cashed that check, you sold your rights." Sammi put Ivan in the cart and then wheeled away. As she whipped up the canned fruit aisle, Anthony approached.

"Hey, was that Helen?"

"Nope."

~ ~ ~ ~ ~ ~ ~

Clowns, riding ponies, an inflatable giant slide and a ball pit were all housed in their backyard. What started as a quaint gathering for family and close friends became the neighborhood block party of the decade.

"Looks like you've put on a little weight, daughter-in-law."

She's ba-ack. "Yes ma'am. Sitting at home with Ivan has packed on a few pounds," she patted her healthy posterior. "Not to worry though. I go back to work in a couple of weeks. It'll all drop off."

Anthony's mother walked to Sammi and sniffed her neck. "No going back to work for you. You're pregnant."

"No I'm not."

"Yes, you are." Mrs. Reid walked away and then returned with Anthony. "Now, tell me again that you're not pregnant."

Sammi looked at her husband and then dropped her head. "What's going on Sammi? Momma said you failed the sniff test." He lifted her head to look into her eyes. "Babe?"

"Dr. Dre said that I was pregnant, but I didn't believe him because all the other doctors said that I couldn't have kids. But now I'm gaining all this weight and my hair is shedding. I didn't want to bother you with this because I thought it was another false alarm, but I think I may actually be pregnant," she blurted without taking a breath. Anthony picked up his wife and spun her around several times. "Babe, you're going to make me throw up. Please put me down."

Sammi spent a lot of time purging her system. Her nose tripled in size, but in her favor, the swelled appendage matched the rest of her body. She had gained over sixty pounds and mustered up hormonal swings that caused Anthony, Rosa and Ivan to take cover. Stretch marks mimicked the map of Ohio and marked the roads to her pooched outie. Miserable.

~ ~ ~ ~ ~ ~ ~ ~

Ivan darted across the room and yanked the privacy drape in the recovery room. He lifted his feet and rode the sliding tapestry like a flying carpet.

"Ivan Anthony Reid, get over here," Anthony said as he chased his son.

"He's awful fast for eighteen months," Nurse Deena said as she checked Sammi's vitals.

"Yeah, he's got my long legs. That's for sure."

"So what name have you chosen for your baby?" She stuck the thermometer in Sammi's mouth.

"Mmmm."

"I like that. You know it means laughter, right?" She removed the device and recorded the temperature on her chart.

"Yeah, I laughed hysterically when the doctor first told me I was pregnant. But today, now that's a different story. I can't think of one aspect of labor and delivery that's funny."

"How about the way you jumped straight up in the stirrups when you had a contraction? Now that was funny." He slapped his knee and laughed until he cried. "I got it all on video."

Sammi glared at her husband. "That's not funny."

"I'll submit it to *America's Funniest Home Videos.* Maybe we'll win the cash prize." He wiped the joy juice from his cheeks.

"I said that's not funny."

"Okay," he covered his mouth and turned away.

"Do you think Ivan will have a problem adjusting to his new brother?"

"Well, we've been talking to him about it for a while and we let him touch my stomach all the time. He got a kick out of watching the ripples run through it."

Ivan ran to the bed and tried to climb up the side rail. "Momma, baby."

"What's he saying?" Nurse Deena folded the arm cuff and tucked it in the monitor.

"He wants his baby. Can you bring Isaac to me?"

"Sure. Give me a few minutes to check on a couple more patients and I'll bring him right in."

"Thanks."

~ ~ ~ ~ ~ ~ ~

"Tee, can you believe that Isaac will be two years old next month?" Sammi said as she opened the pantry door.

"Yeah, time really went fast." He sorted through the mail on the counter.

"I want to give him a big party this year."

"What? The fifty kids at Chuck E. Cheese wasn't big enough?"

"He was afraid of that six-foot mouse, so I want to do something at the house."

"Your wish is my command." He swung his right arm to his waist and bowed. With his face upturned, he said, "How would you like me to assist, madam?"

"Cute. How about you pull the guest list together and get the invitations printed? I'll take care of the rest."

He stood, crossed his arms over his chest and bobbed his head like the wish-granting genie in Aladdin's lamp. "Done."

Three weeks later, the house was full of kids from four months to six years old. The magician had them all captivated with his slight of hand antics. Some of the parents seemed to be mesmerized too. Sammi and Rosa ran from room to room with trays of appetizers, as Anthony played doorman.

"Sammi, look who's here," Anthony said as he entered the family room.

Ivan ran to the latest arrival and wrapped himself around her legs. "Hi, Aunty!"

The tray of appetizers crashed to the floor. Sammi knelt to pick up the spread of finger sandwiches and desserts from My Sweet Cakes. "What is she doing here?" she said without moving her lips. "Who invited her?"

"I figured you did." He squatted to help his wife clean up the mess.

"No, I didn't," she looked up at the newest party guest. "Hi, Helen. What can we do for you?"

"Nothing. I just came to celebrate with my family." Some of the guests whispered. Several moms gathered their children and then walked out of the room.

"Rosa, please get the boys and take the guests outside." Sammi stood and wiped her hands on the clown apron draped around her waist. "I'm going to have to ask you to leave."

"Sorry. No can do," she stepped around Sammi.

Anthony moved toward her. "My wife asked you nicely. You need to leave now."

"Now why are you playing hard to get all of a sudden?" Helen rubbed his arms.

"Excuse me?" He removed her wandering hands from his bulging biceps.

"You didn't tell her?"

"Tell me what?"

"Oops." She threw her hand over her mouth and batted her eyes. "Was that our secret?"

Sammi pushed Anthony back and stood in front of Helen. "I know what you're trying to do and it won't work. Now I've asked you nicely to leave my house." She moved in and stood inches from Helen's face. "It's only by the grace of God that I have not helped you to the door. But if you're not out of here by the time I count to ten," she pulled off her diamond earrings and slipped out of her Prada shoes. "I will jump out of the spirit and into the flesh." She threw up her hand to start the count. "One."

"Babe?"

"Two." Sammi gestured the peace sign with no intentions of surrendering.

Helen placed her hands on her hips and twisted her lips. "Three, four, five." Anthony grabbed Helen's arm and pulled her to the nearest exit. "Let me go. I want to see what ten looks like."

"No, really you don't." He tightened his grip and hastened the pace.

Helen turned her head back toward Sammi. "Since you have your own child, give me mine back! I already had your husband, might as well take your son too!"

"Ten!" Sammi charged at Helen like a bull to a matador. Anthony whisked her out the front door and into the long arm of the law. Their neighbor, Officer Witcher, clanked handcuffs on Helen's wrists, as Sammi ran out the door.

"Ma'am, you're under arrest."

"For what?"

"Trespassing."

"But he let me in," she used her head to point at Anthony.

"Once you were asked to leave, your invitation was revoked." He turned to Anthony. "Sorry it took so long to get here. I was cutting the grass when Rosa called."

"Your timing was perfect."

~ ~ ~ ~ ~ ~ ~ ~

After their bath, Sammi dressed the boys in matching Spider Man pajamas. They bounced on their racecar beds.

"Okay, guys. Time for bed," Anthony said as he joined his family.

"Aw, Daddy. Can we play?" Ivan, the rowdier of the two, attempted a somersault in mid-bounce. Sammi caught him before he hit the wall.

"Not tonight, sweetie," she wiped the sweat from her bangs. "Mommy's tired." She placed her son on the floor. "It's time for prayer." Isaac plopped down next to them.

"Whose turn is it tonight?" Anthony asked as he knelt. "Aagh. My knees don't work like they used to."

"Tell me about it."

"It's my turn," Ivan said. He clasped his hands together. "Close your eyes, Mommy. Thank You God for Mommy and Daddy and Isaac and Mema and Papa and Bebe and Rosa." He opened his right eye. "And thank You for Aunty Helen. In the name of Jesus."

In unison, the family said, "Amen."

Sammi and Anthony kissed their boys and left the door cracked. Anthony walked behind his wife and massaged her neck as they entered their sanctuary.

"We need to keep Helen in our prayers too," he said, as he slid under the covers.

220

"Yeah. She's got a lot of pent-up anger," she leaned over to kiss her king. "And she has sent us through a lot of changes over the years. But I'd do it all over again to keep my family. I can't imagine life without the boys." Sammi rested her head on Anthony's chest and snuggled under his arm. "Let's make a promise."

"Sure. I promise to love you and the boys forever."

"That's not a promise, that's a given," she chuckled. "Let's promise that we'll never tell Ivan about his birth mother. I want the boys to be raised as brothers. Not half-brothers, just brothers."

Anthony shifted his body to look into his wife's eyes. "Wasn't that a given?"

Reflections

External influences create internal chaos.

> Valerie L. Coleman
> Dayton, Ohio
> Penofthewriter.com

When it comes to blended families, remember that life is based on change. The better one is prepared to deal with this fact, the better one will be equipped to handle this major transitional phase of their life.

> Lamarr Lewis
> Dayton, Ohio
> L-marr.com

The parents need to agree upon the methods of disciplining the children. Also, before chastising a child, the parent and child must first establish a relationship. Premature discipline may stifle a healthy relationship and evoke retaliation from the child. Children respond better to discipline when love precedes correction (Ecclesiastes 4:9).

> LaShawn and Joy Lewis
> Moraine, Ohio

Couples bring their life experiences into marriage. Your spouse's style of parenting may differ considerably from yours, good or bad. So to prevent problems, talk through everything from discipline to philosophies on education. One thing is for sure — you cannot be too prepared when it comes to raising children.

> Deena Miller
> Atlanta, Georgia
> Warmspirit.org/deena

The married couple must establish, monitor and enforce rules specific to their household. These rules apply to all the children even if they do not reside in the home. Consistency, reinforcement and agreement are critical to the success of blending families.

Tammy Kessler
Dayton, Ohio

Get to know the biological mother first. If she is crazy like my kids' mom, RUN!

Laura Phillips

Love and accept the new additions to your family as you do your biological children. What you do for yours, you do for all. In our family, we refer to the children as "ours," not "his" or "mine." As in any environment, it is so important to make people feel included and accepted.

Veronica A. Grabill
Centerville, Ohio
Gwlandtitle.com

Remember that more than one way exists to do things. Respect each other's point of view. Look at things from their perspective. Your perception of a situation may differ totally and both ways could be right. Be flexible. No one is perfect except Christ Jesus. Love with all your heart and soul, like the love God has for us.

Debie Lynne Reid
Trotwood, Ohio

Marrying someone who has children is a tricky situation to entertain. Confidence, compassion, understanding, patience, sacrifice, security, acceptance and the ability to recite (and believe in) the Serenity Prayer on a daily basis are great considerations and prerequisites before treading there.

Lyn Handler
Sebring, Florida

Get rid of the words "step" and "half" when talking about family. People are not steps to be trampled upon, nor did God half complete a job!

Rhonda O'Neal
Trotwood, Ohio

Seek the Lord before you marry and let Him guide you. Because you will be marrying your mate, their children and an extended family of parents, grandparents and more, make sure that your marriage is His will and not your own.

Loraine J. Matthews
Dayton, Ohio

Long-term success of a marriage can only be achieved if the marriage is the center of the household. All of the children must understand and respect the marriage as the nucleus of the family. Although they may not always exhibit agreement, children rely on the stability and security of a marriage-centered home. Long after the children are grown and gone, the marriage remains.

Tammy Kessler
Dayton, Ohio

A StepHero™ uses courage, a strong sense of self and a no-matter-what attitude to build a healthy blended family. Tools that make your journey more enjoyable are: an underlying sense of gratitude, a trusted support system, a deep friendship with your partner and an acceptance of your reality.

Emily Bouchard, M.S.S.W.
Rapid City, South Dakota
Blended-families.com

Stepparenting is like working at a late-night convenience store — all of the responsibility and none of the authority.

Valerie L. Coleman
Penofthewriter.com

When families with children blend, the parents need to set new rules and decide how the family will be managed. Each parent hopes to keep things as consistent and safe for their own children as possible. Identifying specific areas of differences, stating clearly what those differences are and working to find common ground is essential for successful family blending.

Marilyn Barnicke Belleghem, M.Ed.
Burlington, Ontario Canada
Questpublishing.ca

Know your place. As the wife, God has called you to be a helpmate. That help may consist of standing in the shadows and allowing your husband to have quality time with his biological children when they come to visit.

Ronelle Kinney
Huber Heights, Ohio

When God's love is present, only a small part of our human struggle will present itself. Notice I did not leave out struggle. A well-blended family makes continuous improvements. Blending for a smoothie or a rocky road is the choice each member of the family must make.

Marcella Ashe
Dayton, Ohio
Allecrampublishing.com

God does not limit us. We limit ourselves with our lack of faith.

Rose Najea
Detroit, Michigan
Najeaenterprises.com

Don't put your mate in the position to have to choose between you and his or her biological children. You may not like the outcome.

Valerie L. Coleman
Penofthewriter.com

I spent ten years growing into the stewardship that God had prepared for my life. What I thought were mistakes have evolved into my blended family. At times stirred, but not shaken.

Marie Moore
Dayton, Ohio

Proverbs 22:6 instructs parents to train up a child. When the stepparent administers discipline in the absence of the biological parent, it is imperative that the chastisement is supported. For example, if dessert is withheld because the child refused to eat dinner, both parents must reinforce the decision.

Sheree Welch
Dayton, Ohio

Entering into a loving marriage with a husband that has a ready-made family has pitfalls that the bride-to-be cannot possibly predict. Your husband, his children and their mother will become a part of your daily life. Remember, even though you are outnumbered by them you have a say on what goes on in your own home.

Monica Morton
New York, New York

Make sure that this is what you want and that you're ready for what lies ahead. Being a stepparent is hard — much is expected of you, but in the end it's never good enough.

Laura Phillips

Maintaining equity in our blended family was like being on a scale. I stood on one side trying to make sure that my children's needs were met and my husband stood on the other side with his children. As I saw the scale tilting in their favor, I added a little more weight (pressure on the marriage) to balance it out. Over time, it only served to burden the relationship. Here's my advice — get off the scale (I do not mean divorce) and quit vying for position in the relationship.

Valerie L. Coleman
Penofthewriter.com

Every bash to a biological parent is a self-inflicted wound. Don't waste energy and negative emotions judging them. Just be the best stepparent you can be.

Lyn Handler
Sebring, Florida

Foremost, Jesus Christ must be first in the parents' lives. Next, the parents must love each other unconditionally. This agape love covers not only their spouse's faults, but the children as well. And last, the parents must possess the fruit of the Spirit (Galatians 5:22–26). Without these ingredients, the family cannot function properly.

Miracle Troutman
Dayton, Ohio

Stop! There's a time and purpose for everything and you may not want to fulfill this purpose. Seriously, in the beginning of the marriage, you must work together to develop expected behaviors and household duties for the children. Also, allow your spouse to discipline the children.

Brenda Wilson
Miamisburg, Ohio

Don't let the other parent run your house! The married couple must establish the rules of engagement for visitations, drop offs, pick ups and vacations, then stick to them. Given the opportunity, the other parent may try to use the children to manipulate your spouse, causing division in the marriage.

Tonya Baker
Clayton, Ohio
Tonyabaker.com

I tried to make my husband make his daughter like me. After ten years of failed attempts, I decided to make myself change.

Valerie L. Coleman
Penofthewriter.com

Perfect Blended Family Recipe – You will need:
o a pinch of timidity or shyness whichever you have on hand
o several barrels of faith
o a heap of creativity
o a couple shakes of self-confidence
Blend in love and mix well. Allow to co-exist. Fill with the Word of God (absolutely no substitutions). Top with prayer.

> Marie Moore
> Dayton, Ohio

Preparation is the key. My son had been solely dependant on me for eleven years and we had grown accustomed to our lifestyle. My fiancé did not have any biological children, so with marriage on the horizon, we sought spiritual counseling. To further assist the transition, my husband took parenting classes through Project Impact. The counseling and classes prepared us for the many adjustments of blending.

> Cheli Chappell
> Dayton, Ohio

Unity is the key to the success of the blended family. Both parents must agree to become and stay unified while raising the children. Children will try to divide the family, if given the opportunity. The Word of God is true and must be applied to our lives daily. *Can two walk together, except they are agreed?* Amos 3:3

> Melvin Williams
> Dayton, Ohio

My daddy taught me that a real gentleman comes to the front door and waits inside instead of honking his car horn. I guess I've turned my husband into a heathen because I'd rather have him wait in the car for his kids than sit in the house with his ex.

> Valerie L. Coleman
> Penofthewriter.com

We forget that God adopted us into the family of Abraham, through our faith in Jesus Christ. This acceptance allows us to receive the rights and privileges afforded to any bloodline descendant of Abraham. When I get to Heaven, I don't want God to say, "This is my stepchild." I want to hear, "This is my child!"

Kevin Scroggins

Attend premarital counseling because you can expect to have problems while the family blends. Put God first, don't try to make your spouse choose between you and the children, and always remember why you fell in love.

Rebecca Simmons
Montclair, New Jersey
Rebeccasimmons.com

God loves us no matter what we do and He commanded us to love our brethren. That love includes the children in our blended families. We must have agapé or unconditional love for the person God created and build genuine relationships through quality time. Otherwise, we hinder our spiritual prosperity.

Bridget Johnson
Huber Heights, Ohio

Foster parenting is a 24-7, 365-days-a-year job. Most often, the biological families have abandoned, abused and neglected their children. The children have no reason to trust you and will intentionally do things to test if you will also abandon them. Your only weapon is unconditional love.

Gwendolyn Cox
Trotwood, Ohio

Trying to make someone love you is like trying to climb uphill during an avalanche.

Valerie L. Coleman
Penofthewriter.com

Put Christ as the head of the family and spend time together as a couple. We lead such busy lives and couple time can slip away or be compromised for other things.

Marti Patterson
Niceville, Florida

Quality family time doesn't have to be a major event. Choose one night a month for dinner and fun. It improves the quality of life and gives children a sense of family identity. In no time at all, your crew will be looking forward to The Funky Family Fun Night.

Patricia Griffin
Dayton, Ohio

Our experiences as children help to formulate our interaction as parents with our own children. Abandonment, insecurity and selfishness are generational curses that must be broken if we are to be effective parents.

Valerie L. Coleman
Penofthewriter.com

~ ~

If this book has been a blessing to you, please let us know. Post your comments at Amazon.com and share your words of wisdom, favorite Scriptures and prayers at Penofthewriter.com.

We also invite you to send us stories for our future anthologies: *Tainted Mirror A Prison Anthology* (Passionate Pens Imprint 2007) and *Blended Families An Anthology Volume 2* (2008).

Pen Of The Writer, LLC
PMB 175 – 5523 Salem Avenue
Dayton, Ohio 45426
info@penofthewriter.com
Penofthewriter.com

~ ~ *About Valerie L. Coleman* ~ ~

Valerie L. Coleman has been called to help writers get their books published. Walking in her purpose, she helped to establish Butterfly Press, a publishing company for Christian books and plays. Valerie has since spread her wings and established her own company, **Pen Of** the **WritER or POWER.**

Valerie has coached hundreds of aspiring authors through the process of writing and publishing. And with a heart to teach and serve, she founded the **Pen To Paper Literary Symposium** in 2004. Past presenters include national best-selling authors Dan Poynter and Kendra Norman-Bellamy. In 2005, Valerie co-founded **Write On! Workshops** with Wendy Hart Beckman and Rhonda Bogan.

Valerie is a contributing writer for *The Midnight Clear*, a Christian fiction anthology published by KNB-Publications. Her story, *Safe in His Arms*, will be included with authors such as Kendra Norman-Bellamy, Patricia Haley and Tia McCollors. In addition, Valerie's story, *His Number One Girl*, has been selected for inclusion in *Chicken Soup for the Stepfamily Soul*.

May 2006, Valerie took her writing and publishing curriculum to the prisons. In addition, she developed the **Passionate Pens** program for high school students. Under her tutelage, students will learn the art and business of writing with the objective of publishing a novella.

Valerie has a bachelor's degree in industrial engineering from GMI Engineering & Management Institute and an MBA from the University of Dayton. She is a senior engineer in the automotive industry and a mathematics instructor for two colleges. A mother of five, she resides in Dayton, Ohio, with her husband, Craig. They worship at Revival Center Ministries, International.

~ ~ *About the Contributors* ~ ~

Wendy Hart Beckman is an award-winning freelance writer and editor. She has been blessed with three sons and her wonderful husband of eighteen years. Her books include *Artists and Writers of the Harlem Renaissance* (Enslow 2002), *National Parks in Crisis: Debating the Issues* (Enslow 2004), *Communication Tools Made Easy* (Kendall/Hunt 2004) and *Dating, Relationships, and Sexuality: What Teens Should Know* (Enslow). Wendy has a master's degree in English—with a concentration in editing and publishing—and a graduate certificate in professional writing from the University of Cincinnati.

Antwonette Marie Caddell, mother of two daughters, works in medical billing during the day. She started writing in church when she tired of the repetitive Christmas play performance. Dared by a Sunday school teacher to write something better, she stepped to the challenge and now writes a new play every year. Antwonette has long desired to be a published author.

Craig Coleman, Sr. is a corrections officer, U.S. Army Reserves sergeant and Pre-Paid Legal independent associate, but more important — he is a man of God. He and his family attend Revival Center Ministries, International. Committed to winning souls for Christ, Craig is a deacon and volunteer van driver for Project Impact. Craig and his wife, Valerie, are marriage coaches for 1ne Ministry. Craig is blessed to have five wonderful children. He penned his first published works for this book. Email: craigppl@aol.com

Dr. Vivi Monroe Congress is the author of *The Bankrupt Spirit: Principles For Turning Setbacks Into Comebacks* and founder of The Grand Prairie African American AUTHOR SHOWCASE. In Fall 2006, she joins an impressive lineup of Christian writers, Anointed Authors On Tour, with book signings in Atlanta, Dallas, Baltimore and other cities. littlelightprod.com/authorshowcase info@littlelightprod.com anointedauthorsontour.com drvivimonroecongress.com

Gwendolyn Cox and her husband, Lawrence, are special treatment foster parents. They serve on the Foster Parent Advisory Board of Agape for Youth, Inc. Since 1998, they have fostered twenty academically challenged, delinquent teenage boys, caring for five at a time. The Coxes help at-risk male teens break family curses by teaching them conflict resolution skills and accountability, and they instill a desire to excel. Gwen and Lawrence are faithful members of Revival Center Ministries, International. GwendolynMCox@aol.com

Veronica A. Grabill grew up in Chicago and attended Northeastern Illinois University. She received her master's degree from Christian Life School of Theology and is working toward her doctoral degree from Beacon University. Veronica was ordained by Pastor Claude Robold of New Covenant Church in Middletown, Ohio and is licensed by the State of Ohio. Veronica mentors young ladies incarcerated in Warren County Juvenile Detention Center. Veronica is married to Vic and they have four children.

Lucinda "Syndi" Greene is a native of Hamilton, Ohio. Syndi attends Revival Center Ministries, International. She writes gospel album reviews for the online Internet site Gospelxone.com. Syndi's expertise in the arts and entertainment industry are utilized by Pen Of The Writer where she acts as assistant publicist, reviewer and bookstore manager.

R. Wade Harper is a graduate of Tennessee State University and works as a manufacturing engineer in the automotive industry. Wade is president of his consultant firm, Precision Insight Manufacturing Services. He is also president and founder of the Computer Guild for Education of Elderly and Kids (GEEK), a non-profit organization that donates gently used, refurbished computers. In his wilderness experience, he wrote *A Gentlemen's Agreement*. If you question what good ever came out of the wilderness, Jesus did!

Wendy E. (Bond) Hayes is a native of Chicago, Illinois. She has a bachelor's degree in civil engineering from Carnegie-Mellon University and a master's degree in manufacturing management from Kettering University. Wendy co-founded the

Why We Sing Gospel Music and Arts Workshop. She resides in Dayton, Ohio with her husband, Rev. Frederick A. Hayes, Sr. and their three children, Iesha, Frederick, Jr. and Taylor.

Benjamin Hicks founded Ingleside Press. His poetry has been published in four anthologies. He self-published several books of poetry: *Life Conflictions* (1995), *Distinguished Young Black Poet: Vol. 1* (1996), *Diary Of Black Love* (1998), *Christmas Poems* (1998) and *Sex Crazy* (2003). His children's books include *Arithmecation* (2003) and *Bryon's Tie* (releases Fall 2006). Benjamin has a bachelor's degree in mass communication from Towson University. He resides in Baltimore and works for Baltimore City Community College. geocities.com/inglesidepressmd

Carolyn Howard-Carnegie is a native Daytonian. She celebrates eighteen years of marriage to her husband, Jimmy L. Carnegie. Carolyn and Jimmy have been blessed with a blended family that consists of three sons and two daughters. Carolyn has been walking with the Lord for fifteen years and truly loves being a friend of God. The family worships at Revival Center Ministries, International in Dayton, Ohio, where she serves on several auxiliaries.

Joshua M. Johnson, CFP®, RFC is the President of Grace Financial Group. He is a certified financial planner® and a registered financial consultant. His specialties are advanced financial, retirement and estate planning. Joshua's desire to educate others has driven him to facilitate hundreds of educational workshops. Joshua enjoys quality time with his wife, Bridget, and their three sons, Brian, Isaiah and Gabriel. He is an active member of Revival Center Ministries, International, serving as a member of the Board of Deacons and Finance Committee. grace-financial.com

Born and raised in Columbus, Ohio, **Karen M. Johnson** is a twenty-year insurance industry professional. She is an avid reader and co-founder of the Ebony Ladies Literary Experience (E.L.L.E.) book club. Karen, a business administration graduate of Ohio Dominican University, resides with her two teenaged children. She is focused on pursuing a writing career and starting a publishing company. *The Years Sown in Tears* is her first published work.

Kevin Wayne Johnson lives in Clarksville, Maryland, with his wife, Gail and three sons, Kevin, Christopher, and Cameron. He authored the nine-book series, *Give God the Glory!*, received multiple literary awards and hosted the *Give God the Glory!* talk show on Voice America Internet Talk Radio Network (voiceamerica.com). He hosts the *Give God the Glory!* television show that is Web cast weekly at blacktvonline.com. He attests everyday that God uses ordinary people to accomplish extraordinary things!

Michelle Larks is an Illinois native. Born and raised in the Windy City, she resides in a western suburb. Educated in the Chicago public school system, Michelle attended the University of Illinois at Chicago. Since 2003, Michelle has released four books: *A Myriad of Emotions*, *Crisis Mode*, *Mirrored Images* (e-book) and *Who's Your Daddy?*. Michellelarks.com

Brenda McKinney, M. S., L. S. W., began her career as a youth counselor at her church. She later obtained a bachelor's degree in social work and a master's degree in counseling. Brenda is a licensed social worker and provides behavioral health counseling / therapy for children, youth, groups and families. She has two daughters and two grandchildren. Brenda resides in Dayton, Ohio and attends Revival Center Ministries, International.

Vanessa Miller of Dayton, Ohio, believes that her God-given destiny is to write and produce plays and novels that bring deliverance to God's people. Vanessa is promoting the first four novels in the seven-book Rain Series: *Former Rain, Abundant Rain, Latter Rain* and *Rain Storm* and has earned several awards for her writing. She is a devoted Christian and mother of Erin. She graduated from Capital University with a degree in organizational communication. Vanessamiller.com

Ordained in her ministry at Revival Center Ministries, International, **Deborah Ogletree** volunteers as the Deaconess

Board administrator and instructor for the New Members Orientation class. A professional sales consultant with an international organization, mother and grandmother, she reads and writes as a hobby. Deborah is focusing her writing interests toward variations of the family structure. The submission, *My Baby's Daddy*, is her first published work. For information on her adoption experience, contact Deborah at: PO Box 20471 Dayton, Ohio 45420 937.219.5846

Idrissa Uqdah, a writer from New Jersey, grew up in Philadelphia. Her fiction and poetry was first published in the 1970s with more recent work in the anthology, *The Heart of Our Community*. She writes book reviews for The Romer Review and Black Literature.com and is a staff writer for BAHIYAH Women Magazine. Idrissa provides communication services for churches and ministry groups. She is working on her debut novel and a collection of short stories.

Lisa Vaughn has been married to Anthony for nine years. Their blended family includes Chris, LaShonna and Carlisa. Together, Lisa and Anthony teach *Altar Workers Ministry* at Revival Center Ministries, International to ensure effective salvation witnessing. Lisa has inspired women to trust God for their marriages and cover their husbands in prayer. In 2007, she will release her nonfiction workbook for altar workers and conduct training seminars. Lisa is a registered nurse at a level one trauma center.

Sonya Visor, co-pastor, author and playwright lives in Racine, Wisconsin with her husband, Pastor Tony Visor, and two sons, Jason and Tony, Jr. She has been a preacher and teacher of the gospel for sixteen years. *The Check for $3.96* is Sonya's first published work. Sonya's book, *Who I've Become Is Not Who I Am,* along with the DVD of her stage production, *Say Amen at the Club*, are available for purchase at Sonyavisor.com.

Recommended Resources

The Stepfamily Foundation
Jeannette Lofas
333 West End Avenue
New York, NY 10023
212.877.3244
Stepfamily.org

Successful Stepfamilies
Ron Deal, LMFT, LPC
SuccessfulStepfamilies.com

Coalition for Marriages
Diane Sollee
5310 Belt Road NW
Washington, DC 20015
202.362.3332
SmartMarriages.com

Blended Families
Emily Bouchard, M.S.S.W.
PO Box 352
Point Roberts, WA 98281
360.945.0250
Blended-Families.com

TheNextWife.com
Paula Enger

Revival Center Ministries, International
Pastors Paul & Keisha Mitchell
3011 Oakridge Drive
Dayton, Ohio 45417
937.263.5226
RevivalCenterMinistriesInternational.org

Attorney Avalon Betts-Gaston
1945 South Halsted Street, Suite 309
Chicago, Illinois 60608

Freelance editors
Wendy Hart Beckman
PO Box 210065
Cincinnati, Ohio 45221-0065

Lynel Johnson Washington
Lmaria23@hotmail.com

Pen Of The Writer

*Out of Ephraim was there a root of them against Amalek; after thee, Benjamin, among thy people; out of Machir came down governors, and out of Zebulun they that handle the **pen of the writer**.*

~ Judges 5:14

Pen Of the WritER

A Christian publishing company committed to using the writing pen as a weapon to fight the enemy and celebrate the good news of Christ Jesus.

Taking writers from pen to paper to published!

Pen Of The Writer, LLC
PMB 175 – 5523 Salem Avenue
Dayton, Ohio 45426
937.307.0760
info@PenOfTheWriter.com
PenOfTheWriter.com

If you liked *Blended Families An Anthology*, you'll love
The Midnight Clear.
ISBN-10: 0-9742207-0-1

With twinkling lights, department store sales, decorated trees, gift exchanges and plump bearded men promising children their hearts' desires, it's no wonder the holiness of Christmas is often lost in the hoopla.

In *The Midnight Clear*, nearly two-dozen authors come together to remind the world of the true meaning of the season. This wonderful assortment of stories will make you laugh, cry and celebrate, as their characters embark on journeys to find gifts of healing, hope and happiness.

Valerie L. Coleman's story, *Safe in His Arms*, deals with a mother's anguish as she spends her first Christmas without her children. Her account is included with some of today's most acclaimed authors of Christian fiction, including Kendra Norman-Bellamy, Patricia Haley, and Tia McCollors.

Quantity	Price	Shipping	Tax*	Total**
	$14.95	$1.99	$1.05	

* Ohio residents add sales tax   ** Money orders only
Order your copy from Pen Of The Writer today!

Name: _____

Address: _____

City / State / Zip: _____

Phone: (_____)_____ Email: _____

If you desire to put your thoughts on paper or you have already put pen to paper, this symposium is for you. Aspiring writers, published authors, book club members and anyone with a passion for literary work will gain insightful knowledge during this intense two-day event.

Day One – The Art of Writing

Mainstream and self-published authors will step you through the process of writing. Genre-specific topics and general sessions will help you hone your craft and catapult your literary works to the next level.

Day Two – The Business of Writing

Seasoned experts will provide practical tools to establish, manage and promote your book business. Attorneys, agents and publishers will enlighten and inspire you to pursue your life passion.

Throughout the day, attendees will have access to printers, editors, web designers, graphic artists and an on-site bookstore. One-on-one critiques by professional editors will give you personalized feedback about your manuscript.

For more information, send inquiries to
Pen To Paper Literary Symposium
PMB 175 – 5523 Salem Avenue
Dayton, Ohio 45426
937.307.0760
info@PenOfTheWriter.com
PenOfTheWriter.com/PenToPaper

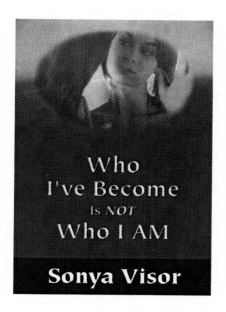

Who I've Become Is *NOT* **Who I AM**

Sonya Visor

Who are you? How did you get here?

We focus too much effort trying to be someone that God never intended only to find ourselves overwhelmed, defeated and depressed.

Sonya teetered on the threshold of death after she tried to construct a person that she was not commissioned to be. *Who I've Become, Is Not Who I Am* explains how our actions and reactions to situations create the illusion of fulfilled life. No longer will you wrestle with the hopelessness of bad decisions, but you'll walk away renewed, refreshed and restored.

Sonya Visor, co-pastor, author and playwright lives with her husband, Pastor Tony Visor, and two sons, Jason and Tony Junior.

P.O. Box 081512
Racine, Wisconsin 53408-1512
Email: Sonya@sonyavisor.com
Sonyavisor.com

Butterfly Press, LLC
Home of *The Rain Series*

Former Rain  Abundant Rain  Latter Rain  Rain Storm

Former Rain was funny, inspirational and moving. This debut novel proves that *The Rain Series* will be a worthy read.
Mahogany Book Club*****
Ms. Miller had me from the first page. A welcomed change from the normal Christian books.
The Pensacola Voice*****

Order your copy today!
VanessaMiller.com or *Amazon.com*

Or mail $14.95* + $1.99 shipping per book to:

Butterfly Press
PMB 257 – 5523 Salem Avenue
Dayton, Ohio 45426   937.248.9211
* Ohio residents add $1.05 per book for sales tax

Former Rain	Abundant Rain	Latter Rain	Rain Storm	Order Total

Name: _____

Address: _____

City / State / Zip: _____

Phone: _____ Email: _____

Blended
Families
an anthology
Edited By
Valerie L Coleman

Order additional copies of
Blended Families An Anthology

Pen Of The Writer
PMB 175 – 5523 Salem Avenue
Dayton, Ohio 45426
937.307.0760
PenOfTheWriter.com
info@PenOfTheWriter.com
* * * * * * * * * * * * * * * * * * *
Please mail _____ copies of
Blended Families An Anthology to
** Call about quantity discounts for family ministries **

Name

Address

City / State / Zip

(_____)

Phone

Email

Quantity	Price Per Book	Total
	$14.95	
Sales Tax (Ohio residents add $1.05 per book)		
Shipping ($1.99 first book, $0.99 each add'l)		
Grand Total* (Payable to: POWER Anthology)		

* Money orders only
  Credit card orders accepted by phone or online.

Printed in the United States
68737LVS00002B/463